Colorado Cravings

Recipes and Romance

from the award-winning
Highland Haven Creekside Inn

THE HIGHLAND HAVEN
Creekside Inn

by Gail Riley
with Bette Milleson James

Original watercolors by Pamela Martin McCarville

Contributing photographer Mark Mattivi

Blueline Publishing LLC
Denver, Colorado

Colorado Cravings
Recipes and Romance
from the award-winning
Highland Haven Creekside Inn

Highland Haven Creekside Inn
Evergreen Colorado
www.highlandhaven.com

Designed by Pamela Martin McCarville
www.allusallthetime.com

First Edition
Second Printing
2007

Blueline Publishing LLC
Denver, Colorado
www.bluelinepub.com

Every effort has been made to ascertain the sources of poetry and
prose quoted in this book and to properly credit those sources.

Printed in Mexico by Impresora Donneco,
a subsidiary of RR Donnelley, Chicago, Illinois.

ISBN 0-9776906-1-X

To Patti—
With warm wishes
Tasty Dishes and the
Romance of
Colorado! —Gail

Colorado Cravings

Recipes and Romance

from the award-winning

Highland Haven Creekside Inn

THE
HIGHLAND
HAVEN

Creekside Inn

Colorado Cravings evokes some of the most compelling qualities of life – food, of course, romance, creativity, and nature. These ingredients have been key elements in the success of the Highland Haven, an award-winning Inn in Colorado that has thrived on these principles for close to 30 years.

Five years ago when I first began to work on this book, my wish was to share the peaceful, romantic qualities of the Inn that my husband, Tom Statzell, and I have worked to create since we acquired the modest mountain motel. Now I offer you the fruits of our labor to satisfy your own Colorado cravings.

Because one of the most elemental and powerful cravings is for comfort food, I proudly invite you to share our great collection of recipes. Among our wonderfully fresh and basic recipes, you will not find a 20-ingredient challenge in this book. Our breakfasts and holiday brunches are our specialty, along with party plans that are usable and creative. You will even be able to enjoy your own party! A favorite of mine, and our guests, is the "Wild West Dinner Party."

Craving for time – sweet time – is even more important. Couples need to soothe themselves with an escape, to talk quietly away from all the pressures of home, office and kiddos. Family and friends all need to lovingly reconnect. As you read the room journal entries throughout the book you will see what I mean – they are so tender and honest. Inspiration for you may come from our "Recipes for Romance" pages. I get a catch in my throat every time I read "The Sweetheart Tree."

The true splendor of our Colorado mountains really fulfills our craving for a connection to nature. A hike in this part of the country or simply sitting by our creek brings out the very best in all of us. In *Colorado Cravings*, you'll find beautiful photographs of the natural surroundings of the Inn. Check out the "River Runs Through It Fly-fishing Party." You don't need a river, just some creativity and our mountain recipes. Each season will offer a Rocky Mountain style of entertaining to get you planning something fun.

I hope the book will, in a small way, help fulfill your cravings.

Warmly,

Gail

Table of Contents

Autumn Leaves... and Cozy Firesides 65

Winter Wonderland... and Snowbears 87

The Inn Through the Seasons 117

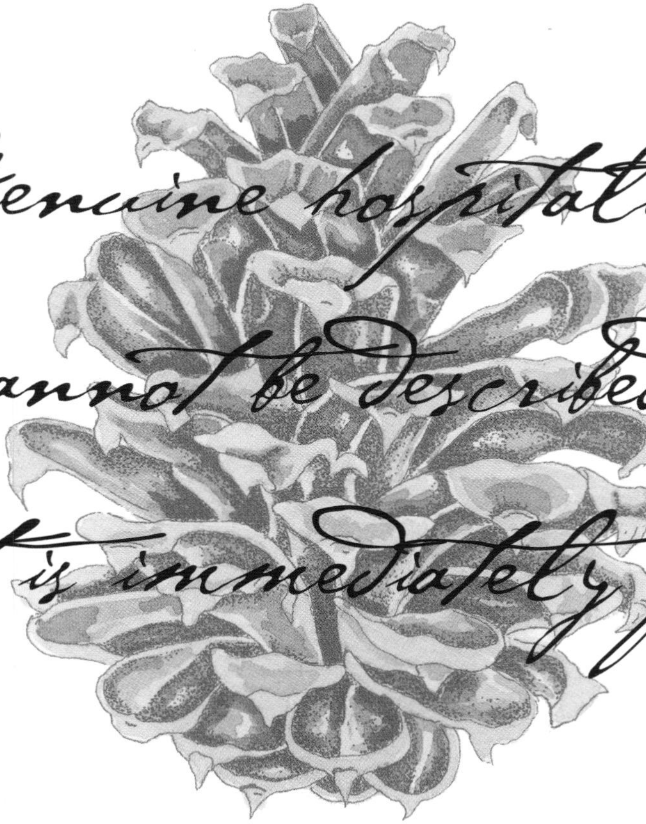

Genuine hospitality cannot be described, but it is immediately felt.

INN
PRIVATE ROAD
GUESTS ONLY
THE HIGHLAND HAVEN
Creekside Inn.
Est. 1961
OPEN YEAR ROUND
Welcome

A Little About the Inn

I want to share what I have learned and created over the years in a practical and beautiful lifestyle book. Collected here are the very best we can offer from years and years of "rattling those pots and pans" in the kitchens of the Inn. This book will inspire other innkeepers, guide gracious hostesses or simply entertain readers hungry for the simplicity and beauty of Rocky Mountain living.

Designed seasonally with creative can-do menus in a "Colorado-chic" style, *Colorado Cravings* will make you swoon over our "A River Runs Through It" summertime fly-fishing party with Bear Creek Smoked Trout Paté, Stuffed Cherry Tomatoes and Spiked Chunky Watermelon. The techniques are not tedious or pretentious but warm and stylish with much room for personal creativity. Here are ways to make our recipes and romance your own as you become the innkeeper of your home. Well-honed skills have proven to be successful for seasons filled with romance, nature and celebrations.

Meet Howard and Mollie at "The Sweetheart Tree." Married for 67 years, they come again and again to the Inn that speaks to them of a kinder and gentler time, inspiring Gail's "Recipes for Romance" or the intimate "Picnic for Just Two." The bevy of brunch offerings will make your mouth water: Miriam's Eggs Eisenhower and Orange Pecan Baked French Toast with a Ramos Fizz Cocktail will inspire you to try them next Sunday.

Colorful photography, original watercolor artwork, quotes of note and touches of history pepper this beautiful and inspired book. Recipes are drawn from actual parties and meals prepared at the Inn, and from friends and family. Try the "High Altitude Tea Party" sans any attitude of stiff traditions: Chive Egg Salad Sandwiches, Cherry Chocolate Scones, and Cranberry Tarts with simply sumptuous ingredients all start with the Viva Glam Champagne cocktail toast to put you and your guests at ease. Add your town's own local specialty foods to make the party your own and impress all. Your girlfriends and family will love this celebration and come to expect the tradition each year.

Your heart will sing and your creative spirits will be lifted as you gather the "ingredients" from the woods to decorate your beautiful flower boxes from autumn through winter. Build a Snow Bear with your little ones, followed by a treat of Minty Cocoa and Eliza's Homemade Graham Crackers to warm your tummies, toes and hearts.

All marked with a sense of imagination and generosity, this book will call you to return to it time and time again. Bring the Rocky Mountain mystique into your home for a style of living that is rich in beauty and full of personal satisfaction.

A Little About Us

I was just 26 when my husband and I bought the ramshackle motel nestled amongst towering blue spruce on a beautiful creek in Evergreen, Colorado. When we first visited before the purchase, we were knocked out by the brilliant blue sky, the huge rock outcropping and all the sunshine. No, we didn't have money. Today I laugh with guests that the sale price of our home wouldn't pave many driveways now. But it was enough to buy the Highland Haven.

My husband worked at odd construction jobs during the day and spent evenings and weekends making much-needed repairs to the motel. I took care of guests and raised two small children.

When Statz and I bought the motel in 1979, it was "stylishly" decorated in shades of harvest gold, avocado green and burnt orange. We collected the twenty-some dollars for the night's rent, handed our guests a key, and hoped with all our might that they would not return with complaints. We, of course, offered no breakfast. Some years later, in an attempt to keep up with the times, we would serve, in our teeny weenie office, a cup of coffee and a cookie as we bid our guests, "Good-bye; have a nice day!"

Ten years later, we brought life back to the main cabin, the Dailey Cabin, in a top-to-bottom restoration. Purportedly the oldest cabin in the canyon, it dates to the mid-1860s and is now the jewel-like anchor of the Highland Haven Creekside Inn. With the restoration came the breakfasts, brunches, holiday parties, fund-raisers, teas, and more.

Now, 27 years after the purchase, by working nearly every day, nearly every week of the year, we have transformed that ramshackle motel into a magical inn.

The refurbished log cabin today is the heart of the Inn; several cabins surround a main lodge. Sparkling Bear Creek runs through the property, which is dotted with massive blue spruce. Elk and deer stroll through our premises regularly to everyone's delight. Bear sightings, fox and an occasional coyote are always special. The Colorado sky is a showcase for the stars and the magic of each season is unmistakably beautiful. The most fortunate part of making this Inn our lifetime job is that we have always been available to our remarkable children, Roxy and Jaxon, who grew up in this wonderful setting and call it home.

As much as our exceptional accommodations, it is our other amenities that keep our guests wanting more: our home-baked breakfasts, specialty parties and champagne celebrations, and the beauty of nature in our lush mountain setting. Awards come at a steady pace now: "Best Mountain Secret," "Best Place to Pop the Question," "Best B and B," "Most Romantic Inn"– Living up to each one keeps us all on our toes.

May golden slumbers
kiss your eyes and may calm await
you when you rise.

Jaxon, Gail, Roxy and Statz

In the Dailey Cabin bathroom we have copies of this favorite passage of ours, rolled, scroll-like, in a little dish for guests to take.

To laugh often and love much,
To win the respect of intelligent people and the affection of children.
To earn the appreciation of honest critics and endure the betrayal of false friends.
To appreciate beauty and to find the best in others.
To give of one's self and to leave the world a little better,
Whether by a healthy child, a garden patch or a redeemed social condition.
To have played and laughed with enthusiasm and sung with exultation.
To know that even one life has breathed easier; this is to have succeeded...

Ralph Waldo Emerson, 1803-1882

The Highland Haven Creekside Inn of Evergreen, Colorado,
welcomes you to brilliant blue skies,
majestic trees, and magnificent wildlife in a charmed location,
nestled on four hundred feet of lulling Bear Creek.

To be 30 miles away
from children, dogs, work...
hardly seems possible.
What an idyllic getaway,
a special 12 hours.
We'll be sure to return.
- guest journal

Our sweet Rowley

The best thing
about owning a dog
is the affection he showers
on us daily.

A Little About Me

Most all I do creatively at the Highland Haven is a result of the inspirations I get from the beauty of nature: colors, lighting, ambience, décor. Nature runs throughout the Inn, in branches, pinecones, twigs, rockwork, birds, art, color. Nearly each week, year 'round, my great pleasure is to call our dog Rowley, grab my red gloves and walking stick, and hike our Fern Gulch woods. I will be calmed, inspired, invigorated, and always I am found to be smiling. The fresh air, warm or cold, the babbling creek, the wildlife, the vistas – all just "send me." Here (and with my family) I am happiest.

Statz and I consider our Highland Haven the vessel for our creativity. We did not enter into this business because we 'like people,' though we certainly do, but as we 'ripen' here we are ever inspired by the opportunities to be creative. We have raised two truly delightful children, and 'blessing' would be the closest word to what this life choice has given us for a very long time. That and love for each other. We are warmed by gratitude daily.

Gail

Even a short stay on your grounds is enough to rekindle one's inner self if only by an early morning walk through the grounds, the pleasure of your extraordinary breakfasts and the warmth generated by the lush and peaceful surroundings of your mountain greenery grounds!
I thank you in advance for the R&R I can once again look forward to enjoying in a few weeks.

Patricia A. Goulding
From a Letter to the Highland Haven

Springtime

Beautiful must be the mountains whence ye come,
And bright the fruitful valleys, the streams,
Wherefrom ye learn your song:
Where are those starry woods? O might I wander there,
Among the flowers, which in that heavenly air
Bloom the year long!

Robert Bridges, 1844-1930

Springtime at the Inn

Love's Philosophy

The fountains mingle with the river
And the rivers with the Ocean.
The winds of heaven mix forever
With a sweet emotion;
Nothing in the world is single;
All things by a law divine
In one spirit meet and mingle,
Why not I with thine? –

See the mountains kiss high heaven
And the waves clasp one another;
No sister-flower would be forgiven
If it disdained its brother;
And the sunlight clasps the earth
And the moonbeams kiss the sea:
What is all this sweet work worth
If thou kiss not me?

Percy Bysshe Shelley, 1792-1822

Romance

- The Sweetheart Tree
- Meet Howard and Mollie
- Recipes for Romance
  - Lynette Champagne
  - Focaccia Bread with Herbed Oil
  - Poached Salmon with Citrus Sauce on Linguini
  - Tropical Fruit Salsa
  - Chocolate Bread Pudding

Romance

Sweetheart Tree in Summer

The Sweetheart Tree

In a prominent spot in front of the Highland Haven, among the oldest and largest blue spruce trees in the Evergreen area, is the Sweetheart Tree, a fifteen-foot stump "topped" by mother nature in the 1980s. There, deeply carved hearts are filled with initials of guests long gone. I tried to make a living as a wood carver in the 1970s, and my carving tools are now loaned to any guest who wants to use them on the tree. Stripped of its bark, the tree has offered memory space to uncounted couples who have visited the inn, many to return again and again. Near the top, an artist has carved a sweet, protective little bear to charm each visitor, and in a high hole safely blessed, a family of pygmy nuthatches has made a home. Pure romance and playful custom, this continuing tradition touches every heart.

The Sweetheart Tree has become a record of lives crossing paths here, and of those whose carvings bring them back again and again to the spot that inspired the hearts and monograms: Holly and Tim's heart was a wedding gift from Statz and me, and in the journal they thank us *"for being a part of the most amazing day of our lives."* One bright carving was a surprise for Statz, in celebration of our 25th anniversary. Honeymooners Monica and Rob have enriched their lives with children and busy schedules, but they still return to visit the tree, to walk around the lake, and to note in their journal, ***"This is the perfect place for romance."*** And from our best friends, one gentle, poignant carving reveals the love of a young son, Matthew, for Peter, the father he has lost, and for Melissa, the mother he wishes to comfort.

Though nothing can bring back the hour
Of splendour in the grass, of glory in the flower;
We will grieve not, rather find
Strength in what remains . . .

William Wordsworth, 1770-1850

Meet Howard and Mollie

A story that warms the heart is that of Howard and Mollie, who have been to the tree many times, most recently to celebrate their 67th wedding anniversary in a place that recalls for them the lifetime spent in the Evergreen area. Through lives changed and changing Howard and Mollie know that *"… nothing can bring back the hour of splendour in the grass, of glory in the flower…"* but, like William Wordsworth, they *"find strength in what remains."*

For them, one place that remains is this Highland Haven, where recently they placed in the Creekside Cottage One journal a notation: *"There's no place like this to spend our anniversary…"*

All these are part of the ongoing story of the heart-filled Sweetheart Tree and the second tree that is now being filled with names and messages. Perhaps Howard and Mollie will have a new heart there. After all, the new tree will reflect young love and old love, family love and fleeting love, past love and love cut short … and the oldest and the deepest love of all, the love that time has tested and found true. *Statz and I delight in being part of these ongoing love stories. There is something magic here.*

To Gail and Staff
For a memorable 96th birthday
I give you a grateful "Thank You."
Not only for the birthday but also for the 80 years
spent in the Evergreen area that
Highland Haven brings back to me.
God Bless you all.

Howard and Mollie Head, Arvada, Colorado - guest journal

Howard & Mollie

Recipes for Romance

You know better than anyone what type of meal will win the heart of the one you love. Is he a "meat and potatoes" guy or would she swoon if you prepared Grilled Scampi in a white wine sauce and risotto? Whatever you prepare, set the mood with your favorite music, an intimate seating in front of the fireplace, outside on the deck or in your bedroom if you like. I like to add the magic of candles, my best dishes and stemware and privacy. Find here an easy and special Dinner for Two that will show your sweetheart that you care.

Tropical Fruit Salsa

1 cup finely chopped pineapple
1 cup chopped mango or papaya
1 cup slivered red onion
1 cup slivered sweet peppers; red, yellow and green
(the more colors the prettier!)
2 tablespoons chopped fresh cilantro
1 teaspoon lemon or lime zest
1 tablespoon lemon or lime juice
1 teaspoon fresh grated ginger (optional)

In a medium bowl, stir together the pineapple, mango or papaya, red onion, sweet peppers, cilantro, lemon or lime zest, lemon or lime juice and ginger.

Cover and chill for 8 to 10 hours.

Poached Salmon with Citrus Sauce on Linguini

2 fillets of fresh or frozen skinless salmon (thaw if frozen)
garlic pepper seasoning
1 cup water
1 cup dry white wine or chicken broth
4-5 ounces linguini (follow directions on package)

Sauce:

2 tablespoons melted butter
2 teaspoons lemon juice
1 tablespoon capers

Prepare sauce and linguini; set aside to reheat when salmon is cooked.

Rub fish fillets with garlic pepper seasoning.

In large skillet bring water to slow boil. Add wine or chicken broth, return to boil.

Add fish, simmer covered 6 minutes per inch thickness of fish. Fish should flake easily with fork.

Remove with slotted spoon.

Place on hot linguini; spoon sauce mixture over salmon and linguini.

Chocolate Bread Pudding with Whiskey Sauce

1 loaf French bread
4 cups milk
2 tablespoons vanilla
3 eggs
1½ cups sugar
1 cup chocolate pieces

Sauce: (optional)

½ cup melted butter
2 tablespoons whiskey

Tear the bread into 1-inch pieces.

Place in large bowl, add milk and vanilla.

Mix and cover to let stand at room temperature for one hour.

Mix eggs, sugar and chocolate pieces together, add to milk and bread mixture and stir well.

Pour into buttered casserole dish and bake at 375° for one hour.

You may serve warm with whiskey butter sauce over top.

Note: See variations of this recipe on page 82.

Last night was the best night of my life. I feel like I'm living a fairy tale.
Our room was cozy and romantic. Highland Haven brings the fairy tale to life.

- guest journal

Menu

Lynette Champagne

Focaccia Bread with Herbed Oil

Poached Salmon with Citrus Sauce on Linguini

Tropical Fruit Salsa

Chocolate Bread Pudding with Warm Sauce

Lynette Champagne

In a champagne flute pour only one tablespoon of Grand Marneir liqueur in each glass.

Top with champagne.

Garnish with a strawberry; float a smaller one or place a big slice on lip of flute.

Cheers!

Focaccia Bread with Herbed Oil

Buy your favorite focaccia bread and serve with a small bowl of your best olive oil sprinkled with garlic salt, pepper and grated Parmesan cheese.

Tea pot is on, the cups are waiting,

Favorite chairs anticipating,

No matter what I have to do,

My friend, there's always time for you.

Anonymous

High Altitude Tea

- Your Favorite Variety of Teas
- Viva Glam Champagne
- Buff Orpington Chive Egg Salad Sandwiches
- Tarragon Chicken Salad Sandwiches
- Teatime Trout Paté
- Citrus Fruit Flower
- Dark Chocolate Cherry Scones
- Our Signature Trifle

High Altitude Tea

High tea in the high country – *festive, inviting, heartwarming* – gives a group of friends time together to talk, to indulge, to reconnect. Our guests love the beautiful setting and mountain menu at the Inn, but you don't need a mountain to make this gesture of friendship, and you don't need weeks of time to prepare these special foods or to adapt the menu to your local cuisine with lovely and inspired creations of your own.

Your guests will feel like Rocky Mountain Royalty in a beautiful, cozy room by a snapping fire, with their every wish anticipated and fulfilled by doting hosts. At the Highland Haven, we offer trout paté, "dolled-up" scones, hearty sandwiches, baked delectables, unique colorful desserts, Colorado chocolates, and a variety of teas that please. In your part of the country, use local products and personal favorites, or follow our mountain menu to the last detail. Either way, your friends will love the atmosphere you offer.

Set the mood for your tea with a beautiful flute of "Viva Glam" champagne, handed to each guest as she arrives. Each beautifully decorated place setting can be enhanced by a charming "folded envelope" napkin with a carefully prepared souvenir menu tucked into the fold. Let instrumental music appropriate to the event come wafting through the room among the friends and the sparkling miniature lights.

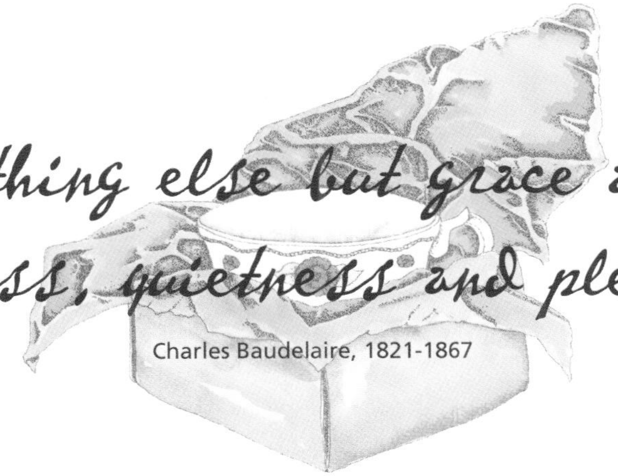

There is nothing else but grace and measure,
richness, quietness and pleasure.

Charles Baudelaire, 1821-1867

At holiday time, focus on grandmas, moms, and daughters, on sisters and aunts and "just like family" friends. Ask each guest to bring a teacup that is dear to her. Have a dear friend prepared to begin a round of teacup memories. Stories of touching moments, funny people, lost days – all these will open the hearts of family and friends to one another, and renew the connections and common hearts among them. After the stories, collect the cups, wash them, and place each in a tissue-lined box, along with a gift of a special little vintage handkerchief or a hand-made commemorative ornament.

This is an idea I had for years before we offered it to our guests
and local friends. I had no intention of comparing my
High Altitude Tea Party to the formal and proper English teas.
Our theme would be true to Colorado… so we offer trout paté,
teas and chocolates from Colorado and
an ambiance that is less formal and more mountain style.
Our sandwiches are heartier and our desserts are very colorful.

When teas and goodies are gone, when teacups are washed and gifted back to the owners, when stories are told and relaxed ambiance abounds and good-byes have been said, your guests will realize anew the value of what Samuel Johnson, more than two hundred years ago, called *"the endearing elegance of female friendship."* After such a day, they'll truly think they've been to a highland heaven.

Gail on the Dailey Cabin's Pioneer Porch

High Altitude Tea Party Colorado Style

Thank you for a taste of simple elegance
exquisitely accomplished.
- guest journal

Buff Orpington Chive Egg Salad Sandwiches

12 thin slices white bread
Unsalted butter – softened
6 hard-cooked eggs
2 tablespoons mayonnaise
1 tablespoon sour cream
¼ cup chopped, seeded, cucumber
2 tablespoons chopped chives
Salt and pepper to taste

Spread the bread lightly with the butter.

Using a shaped metal cookie cutter, cut 12 flowers from bread slices.

In a bowl, chop the eggs.

Stir in the mayonnaise and sour cream.

Fold in the cucumber and chives.

Season with salt and pepper.

Spread the egg salad on the bread cutouts.

Arrange chive blossoms in a circle in the center of each sandwich to resemble a flower.

Tarragon Chicken Salad Sandwiches

1 cup finely chopped cooked chicken
2 tablespoons chopped cucumber
2 tablespoons chopped green bell pepper
1 tablespoon chopped fresh tarragon
1 tablespoon white wine vinegar
1 tablespoon oil
1 tablespoon mayonnaise
2 tablespoons fresh chopped parsley
12 thin slices white or wheat bread, lightly buttered

In a medium-size bowl, combine the chicken, cucumber, green bell pepper and tarragon.

In a small bowl, whisk together the vinegar, oil and mayonnaise until blended.

Stir the dressing into the chicken mixture. Assemble.

Cut each in half.

To garnish, lightly butter top edge of each sandwich and sprinkle lightly with fresh parsley.

Makes 6 sandwiches.

Easter at Highland Haven

- Copa Cocktail
- Cheesy Breakfast Casserole
- Kline Family Ham Balls
- Parmesan Oven Fries
- Blueberry Lattice Coffee Cake

Easter Morning

Pastels of Easter

Easter in Evergreen can offer snowy mornings, or bright sunny days more suitable for the Easter bunny. He, being me, hops out of bed early to beat the guests out their doors. I generally enlist the help of little ones the days before to dye our eggs in a traditional style or use a softer tea dye in shades of amber. An assortment of chocolates and the season's most trendy candy I load in a basket and quietly gift an assortment at each door. A collection hidden on our porch adds a colorful welcome to our hungry guests, rising early to enjoy our knock-out Easter breakfast.

Over the years we have had lovely egg hunts on our front lawn, with colorful eggs tucked under the shrubs amongst the towering blue spruce. Nothing is more fun at Easter than darling kiddos in their Easter finery discovering a gift of candy and eggs.

I thought that one only finds this
peacefulness after one dies.
This is as close to heaven as I've ever been
and if heaven is any less I'll be very disappointed.
- guest journal

I love to do a cute little Easter Egg Hunt on the front lawn among the trees and shrubs, and offer our guests a fabulous Easter Brunch.

Cheesy Breakfast Casserole

10 slices whole-wheat bread torn into thirds
1 medium onion, chopped
1 pound shredded cheddar or Colby cheese
4 eggs, lightly beaten
3 cups milk
1 tablespoon Worcestershire sauce
1 teaspoon dry mustard
½ teaspoon salt
¼ teaspoon pepper

In a pretty greased 2-quart casserole, place ⅓ of the torn pieces of bread. Sprinkle ⅓ of onion and ⅓ of cheese. Repeat layering.

In a 1-quart measuring cup, whisk together the eggs, milk, Worcestershire sauce, mustard, salt and pepper. Pour over bread, onions and cheese. Cover with plastic wrap and refrigerate overnight.

Remove and bring to room temperature for 30 minutes.

Preheat oven to 325°.

Bake for 50-60 minutes. Casserole will come out of oven puffy. It will deflate a bit as it cools.

Easter Breakfast

Parmesan Oven Fries

4 large baking potatoes
1 teaspoon dried parsley
¼ teaspoon pepper
2 tablespoons olive oil
Vegetable cooking spray
¼ cup freshly grated Parmesan cheese
1 teaspoon salt

Cut each potato lengthwise into 8-10 wedges.

Pat wedges dry with paper towel and place in bowl.

Add parsley and pepper; toss well.

Arrange in single layer on a baking sheet coated with cooking spray.

Bake at 450° for 30 minutes.

Sprinkle cheese and salt evenly over wedges. Bake an additional 10 minutes or until tender and brown.

Serve warm. Serves 6.

We serve roast potatoes every day at the Inn and there are countless variations. Since we do "overnight food" we first bake our potatoes until just barely done. We allow them to cool; then we do our magic. Cut in your favorite style: rounds, half rounds, strips, wedges, small chunks. Next coat in your olive oil and add your choice: sliced onions, fresh rosemary (my favorite), garlic salt, parsley or paprika. I mix with clean hands to coat potatoes thoroughly. We cover over night and in the morning bake or quickly fry in a skillet for small batches.

Kline Family Ham Balls

2½ pounds ground lean pork
2 pounds ground cooked ham
1½ cup fine bread crumbs
4 eggs
1 teaspoon salt
¼ teaspoon pepper

Sauce:

¾ cup brown sugar, packed
1 tablespoon dry mustard
⅛ cup vinegar
½ cup water

Combine meat, bread crumbs, eggs and seasonings.

Mix well and shape or scoop into balls.

Place in baking dish.

Combine sauce ingredients and pour over Ham Balls.

Bake for 1 hour at 350°. Makes 36.

You may make a day or night before.
Always a smashing success.

O childhood days enchanted!
O the magic of the Spring!
With all green boughs to blossom white,
and all bluebirds to sing!
When all the air, to toss and quaff,
made life a jubilee
And changed the children's song and
laugh to shrieks of ecstasy.

James Whitcomb Riley, 1849-1916

Carly's Blueberry Lattice Coffeecake

Menu

Copa Cocktail
Cheesy Breakfast Casserole
Kline Family Ham Balls
Parmesan Oven Fries
Blueberry Lattice Coffee Cake

Copa Cocktail

One part champagne
Two parts orange juice
Splash of Cointreau

1 package active dry yeast
1 teaspoon sugar
¼ cup warm water
1 egg beaten
½ cup butter softened
⅓ cup milk
3 cups flour
¼ cup sugar
½ teaspoon salt
16 ounces cream cheese
2 egg yolks
⅔ cup sugar
1 teaspoon vanilla
1 tablespoon grated lemon peel
1 cup fresh or frozen blueberries
powdered sugar

Dissolve yeast and 1 teaspoon sugar in warm water in large bowl. Let stand 10 minutes.

Beat in 1 egg, butter and milk. Beat in flour, ¼ cup sugar and salt to make soft dough. Knead on lightly floured surface about 10 minutes or until smooth and satiny, adding more flour as necessary to prevent sticking. Cover and let rest while making filling.

Combine cream cheese, 2 egg yolks, ⅔ cup sugar, vanilla and lemon peel in medium bowl. Beat until combined; set aside.

Grease 13x9-inch pan, divide dough into thirds; set ⅓ aside. Roll out remaining ⅔ of dough into 13x9-inch rectangle. Place in greased pan and press dough ½ inch up sides to contain filling.

Spoon filling into dough-lined pan. Arrange blueberries over filling, pressing lightly into filling. Roll out remaining dough to 10 inch square. Cut dough into 1 inch strips. Arrange strips diagonally across pan in lattice pattern over filling, sealing strips to edges. Cover with plastic wrap and refrigerate at least 2 hours or overnight.

Preheat oven to 350° and bake, uncovered, about 40 minutes or until lightly browned and filling is set. Serve warm or at room temperature. Sprinkle with powdered sugar when the cake has cooled.

More Spring Recipes

Roasted Potato Wedges

4 Yukon Gold or Russet potatoes
4 tablespoons olive oil
Salt and pepper
2 tablespoons dried parsley flakes

Wash and cut potatoes into 1/2 inch wedges. Dry the potatoes with a towel.

To a heated skillet, add the oil. Add the potatoes, salt and pepper.

Sauté the potatoes for about 3 minutes, stirring to make sure they are well coated with oil.

Transfer to a preheated 350° oven for 30 minutes.

Stir and bake 15 minutes more.

Toss with parsley just before serving.

Gardener's Egg Bake

8 ounces sharp cheddar cheese, grated
1 tablespoon flour
4 ounces Monterey Jack cheese, grated
½ cup half & half
6 eggs, beaten
1 tablespoon Worcestershire sauce
1 medium tomato, chopped
3 tablespoons fresh basil, chopped

Preheat oven to 350°.

Toss grated cheddar cheese with flour.

Place in ungreased casserole (8 inch square or pie plate).

Sprinkle grated jack cheese over top.

Combine half & half and eggs, add Worcestershire sauce, mix well, and pour over cheeses.

Sprinkle chopped tomato and basil over egg mixture and bake for 35 to 40 minutes.

Can be prepared 24 hours in advance of baking.

Serves six to eight.

Cherry Almond Cake

1 cup flour
1 teaspoon baking powder
⅛ teaspoon salt
⅛ teaspoon ground cloves
⅔ cup granulated sugar
3½ tablespoons butter, softened
3 tablespoons low-fat cream cheese
2 tablespoons almond paste
¼ teaspoon almond extract
1 large egg
⅓ cup low-fat milk
cooking spray
2 tablespoons chopped almonds, toasted
2 tablespoons granulated sugar
1 (14.5 ounce) can pitted tart red cherries, drained
1 teaspoon powdered sugar

Combine flour, baking powder, salt and cloves in a small bowl.

Combine granulated sugar with butter, cream cheese, almond paste, almond extract, and egg in a larger bowl. Beat with mixer until well blended.

Add flour mixture and milk alternately to sugar mixture, beginning and ending with flour mixture. Pour batter into a 9-inch round cake pan coated with cooking spray.

Combine almonds and 2 tablespoons granulated sugar; sprinkle over batter. Arrange cherries on top. Bake at 350° for 50 minutes or until a toothpick comes out clean. Cool in pan 10 minutes; remove from pan. Sift powdered sugar over the top.

A cabin with plenty of food is better
than a hungry castle.
Irish Proverb

Got proposed to this day!
Walked in and the flowers were there on the table,
my favorite music was on, wine was chilling!
Walked into the hot tub room and presents were
sprawled on the bed…
the last was a beautiful engagement ring.
Thank you for the ambience.
- guest journal

Decadent Double-Dipped Strawberries

1 pound stemmed strawberries
1 12-ounce package semi-sweet chocolate pieces
6 ounces white chocolate pieces

Wash strawberries and dry completely. Line cookie sheet with waxed paper.

Melt semi-sweet chocolate pieces in a double boiler or microwave. If consistency is too thick, add small mounts of butter to thin out. Dip each berry, covering ¾ of the berry. Place on waxed paper and set in a cool, dry place for 10 minutes.

Melt white chocolate in double boiler or microwave. Stir and check often, as white chocolate burns easily. Scoop white chocolate into a freezer bag. Snip the corner, making a 1/16-inch hole. Use freezer bag as you would a pastry bag to stream chocolate over the berries. Let set again at least 15 minutes before serving.

Note: If making in advance, be sure to store in a cool, dry place. The refrigerator may be too cold and cause cocoa butter to rise out of the chocolate and leave white marks.

It is still difficult for most of the staff to pronounce "Clafouti" (Kla-fowty). But once they taste these concoctions they are not easily forgotten. I love to bake them; they are the perfect blend of fruit and rich custard, and they look wonderful. We serve for brunches at the Inn and they are a fabulous end to a special meal.

Apple-Raisin Clafouti

2 tablespoons butter
4 medium apples, peeled, cored and sliced (about 5 cups)
½ cup raisins (golden are nice too)
½ cup sugar
¼ teaspoon ground nutmeg
⅔ cup flour
½ cup milk
3 eggs
1 tablespoon vanilla
2 tablespoons powdered sugar

Coat 2-quart round casserole or quiche dish with cooking spray. Set aside.

In skillet heat butter over medium heat until melted.

Add apples. Cook and stir over medium-high heat until apples are light brown.

Stir in raisins, 1/4 cup sugar and nutmeg. Spread apple mixture into prepared pan.

In a blender container combine flour, milk, eggs, 1/4 cup sugar and vanilla. Cover and blend on high 1 minute. Pour batter over apple mixture.

Bake in a 350° oven for 55 to 60 minutes or until a toothpick inserted near center comes out clean.

Sprinkle with powdered sugar. Serve warm in pie-shaped servings. Makes 6-8 servings.

Note: Other versions of this recipe are on pages 63 and 79.

Blueberry Crisp

7 cups fresh blueberries
¾ cup sugar
1 tablespoon plus 1⅓ cups flour divided
1 tablespoon fresh lemon juice
¾ cup firmly packed brown sugar
1 teaspoon ground cinnamon
¼ teaspoon salt
1 stick cold butter, cut into pieces
¾ cup chopped pecans

Heat oven to 350°.

In large bowl combine berries, sugar, 1 tablespoon flour and lemon juice.

In medium bowl combine remaining 1⅓ cups flour, brown sugar, cinnamon and salt.

Cut in butter until coarse and crumbly; add pecans.

Spoon berries into square baking dish or quiche pan. Top with brown sugar mixture.

Bake 45 to 50 minutes or until filling is bubbly hot and browned.

Serve warm or room temperature.

Susan's Egg and Green Chili Bake

Combine the following in large bowl:
16 ounces diced green chilies
8 ounces mild cheddar shredded
8 ounces sharp cheddar shredded
12 eggs beaten
16 ounces sour cream
1½ teaspoons salt

Pour into large greased baking dish and bake at 350° for 35-40 minutes.

Serves 8.

Rosemary Garlic Roast Potatoes

4 pounds new potatoes, scrubbed, halved
2 heads of garlic, cloves separated and chopped
4 tablespoons fresh rosemary, chopped
¼ cup olive oil
Kosher salt and pepper to taste

Preheat oven to 400°.

In a large bowl, toss new potatoes and garlic cloves with rosemary.

Toss with olive oil to coat lightly and add salt and pepper to taste.

Lightly oil a sheet-cake pan and spread potatoes out into one layer, cut side down.

Roast for 30-45 minutes or until golden brown and tender.

Remove from oven and let cool for 20 minutes before serving.

Country Soufflé

2 tablespoons butter
3 tablespoons flour
1¼ cups cold milk
¼ teaspoon salt
¼ teaspoon pepper
⅛ teaspoon nutmeg
1½ cups shredded Gruyère cheese
3 eggs
3 tablespoons parsley

Lightly grease a 4-cup oval or square dish.

In a medium saucepan, melt the butter over moderate heat.

Add flour and cook until mixture begins to sizzle, then whisk in the milk and bring to a boil, whisking constantly.

Season the sauce with the salt, pepper and nutmeg and remove from heat.

Let cool slightly, then stir in the cheese, eggs, and parsley.

Bake for 30 to 40 minutes at 400°.

It has been a dream of mine to stay in a place like this. It seems that after reading what others had to say before my stop that God has blessed this place with peacefulness. Thank you for this special time.

- guest journal

Summertime

I needed a place to rejuvenate,
To reclaim my inner peace.
I found it.

- guest journal

Summertime at the Inn

As a native of Colorado
I am proud that we have places like this
to share with people all over the country and world.
This was truly a moment in time we will never forget.
It was a romantic experience for us.
Thanks for being so kind.

- guest journal

"A River Runs Through It" Fly-fishing Party

- Bear Creek Smoked Trout Paté
- Cherry Tomatoes Stuffed with Mozzarella Cheese
- Marinated Button Mushrooms
- Watermelon Slices
- Limeade in Sugar-Rimmed Glasses

Fly-fishing

Gail with friends and guests Kathy and Cathy

Summertime, and the livin' is easy . . . and fun! Your friends will love your "A River Runs Through It" Fly-fishing Party. Have vintage copies of Norman Maclean's classic novel on hand to set the lean-back-and-relax, mountain-hideaway mood of the party. You don't need a creek or Robert Redford to capture the essence, and the special men in your life will love the entire experience. Buy the sound track for Redford's remarkable film, *A River Runs Through It,* put it to good use by setting the musical mood, and try as many as you like of these party enhancements:

★ Use a big bucket or wheelbarrow for your micro-brew beers, soft drinks and waters.

★ Fly white canvas fish flags along the creek if you have one, along your walkway if you don't.

★ Serve classic limeade in big, sugar-rimmed glasses.

★ Make your own ice cream sandwiches and heap them on trays to pass among your guests (directions on page 51).

★ Fill fishing-theme papers with fishing quotes on trout or fly-fishing, the date and place of your party, and your good wishes as a take-home token for your party guests.

★ Ask a local fly-fishing shop to demonstrate casting and fly-tying to guests.

★ Find a friend to start the fish stories *flowing* . . . just ask your guests to bring any photos or stories of fishing tales to share.

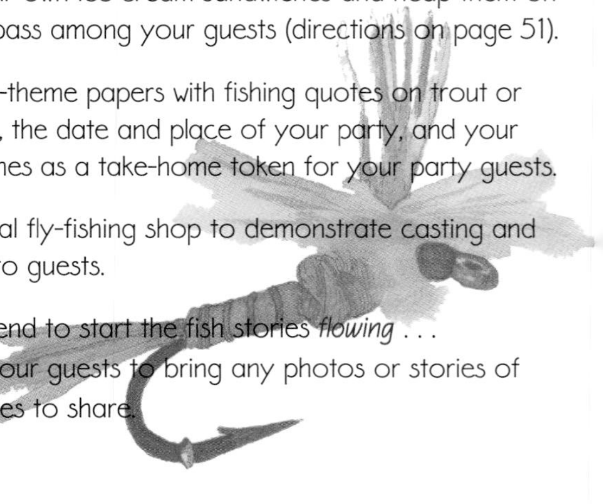

Though the mystical quality of fly-fishing may escape the couch potato, it is a deeply felt and much desired experience for the true flyfisherman. More than a sport, fly-fishing offers a communication with earth, water and sky that makes its aficionados one with the natural world in a transcendental way that seems impossible through any other means. Simply put, there is nothing else like it.

At Highland Haven, and throughout Colorado, fly-fishing and its mystique draw fishermen and naturalists from all over the country, indeed from around the world. For novices, the Blue Quill Angler at Evergreen offers a learning experience second to none. For more experienced enthusiasts who prefer to strike out on their own, the rivers and streams of Colorado are unsurpassed in their rugged beauty and their silver rushing waters, their deep, quiet pools and shaded banks.

Fly-fishing quickly becomes a necessary experience for those who learn to love it – partly for the sport of it, partly for the pride in their acquired skill, and partly for the natural peace that emanates from the beautiful and isolated places where fishing is at its best. The cherished days spent on the river are often gifts given from wives to husbands, or from grandpa to grandson in a shared high-country adventure that offers a bonding for the pair as well as fun for the child.

Early fishermen, less esoteric than today's sometimes particular sportsmen, may have had more motivation in food than in sport or communion with nature, but they were no less enthusiastic. On Bear Creek, just downstream from the Highland Haven, two early nineteenth-century fishermen paused just long enough for this rare vintage photo of a day on the water.

On the other hand, some fishing expeditions are less reverent or purposeful than others. We three women, dressed to the nines for fly-fishing adventure, found our plans abruptly ended by the vagaries of Colorado weather when lightning, never a good fishing companion, entered the picture. I have not, to this day, caught a single fish and I happily live with that fact. I got what I wanted – the outfit, the gear, and the photo – *without even getting wet!*

What is the best part about staying here? A. The rushing river B. The blue spruce C. No little brother. If you guessed C you are correct! If you didn't, you don't have a brother.

- guest journal

*To me the beauty of fly-fishing is just being outdoors in Colorado's beauty.
I am so distracted by the scenery,
I just don't care about catching a fish!*

Bear Creek Fishermen - Photo courtesy of Jefferson County Historical Society

"A River Runs Through It" Party Recipes

Cherry Tomatoes with Mozzarella Filling

40 red, firm cherry tomatoes
½ pound fresh mozzarella cheese
cut into ¼-inch cubes
2 tablespoons chopped sun-dried tomatoes
¼ cup olive oil
Freshly ground black pepper to taste
1 tablespoon chopped fresh basil leaves

Wash and dry the cherry tomatoes.

With a sharp serrated knife, cut off the round bottom of each tomato. Remove the stem, seeds and pulp with a small melon-ball scoop and put the tomatoes, cut-side down, on a rack or paper towels to drain.

Refrigerate until ready to use.

Marinate the cheese and sun-dried tomatoes in the olive oil and pepper for several hours before stuffing into the tomatoes. Sprinkle with basil.

Marinated Mushrooms

1 pound medium or small mushrooms
2 tablespoons sherry vinegar
1 tablespoon Balsamic vinegar
1 tablespoon freshly ground black pepper
½ cup olive oil
2 tablespoons small capers

Trim the stems of the mushrooms and wipe the caps clean with a damp towel.

Combine the vinegars, pepper, oil and capers in a mixing bowl.

Toss in the mushrooms and marinate covered for 3 hours up to overnight.

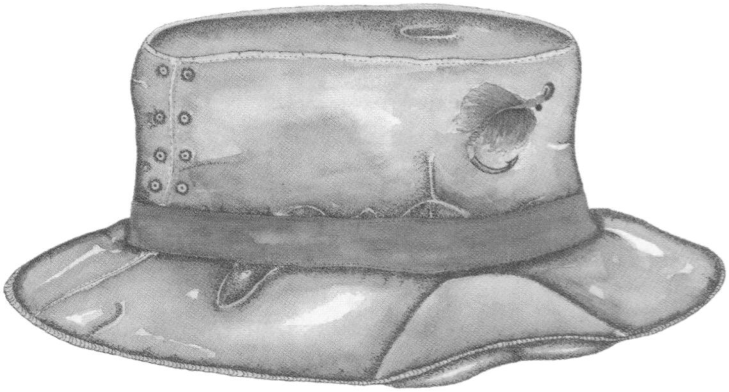

Bear Creek Smoked Trout Paté

12 ounces smoked trout (boned, crumbled)
1 cup cream cheese
1 cup cottage cheese
1 teaspoon horseradish
1 teaspoon lemon juice
pepper
1 tablespoon chopped parsley
1 tablespoon bread crumbs
paprika
2 tablespoons diced red onion
2 tablespoons capers

Place fish, cheeses, horseradish and lemon juice in a food processor or blender and mix until smooth.

Season with pepper, add parsley and bread crumbs and blend together.

Line fish mold (or simply use a small bowl) with plastic wrap. Press into mold and cover and chill for 8 hours.

Unmold onto serving plate. Garnish with capers and diced red onion. Lightly sprinkle with paprika for color.

Serve with toast points, baguettes, or crackers.

Note: If you don't have a mold you like, it is easy to shape a fish by hand. You can shape the gills, use capers for the eyes and make an impressive presentation on a platter of decorative lettuce. Make scales with cucumber or onion half rounds.

I have laid aside business, and gone a-fishing.

Izaak Walton, 1593-1683

Menu

Bear Creek
Smoked Trout Paté

Cherry Tomatoes Stuffed
with Mozzarella Cheese

Marinated Button Mushrooms

Watermelon Slices

Limeade in
Sugar-Rimmed Glasses

Sugar-Rimmed Glasses

Create your own color or shade. Coarse sugar has a more dramatic effect.

1 cup of sugar
Food color as needed

In a small bowl combine sugar and food color. You will need to work in the color with a spoon.

Dip glass in bowl of water 1/8 inch from the top of rim all the way around.
Press into sugar. You will need to make sure that all the water saturated the sugar – otherwise this will run down the side of the glass.
Pour in freshly squeezed limeade sugared to taste or simply add crushed ice to a frozen blend.

The world's less about assembly lines from where I sit
and a lot more about graceful lines.
From where I sit I can touch another time while still
very much in the present.
From here, I can rest my body and exercise my mind.
From where I sit, the possibilities are endless.

Anonymous

Garden Patch Party

- Tropical Fruit Salsa
- Grilled Lemon Chicken
- Fried Green Tomatoes
- Spiked Watermelon
- Cone Fruit Tree
- Ice Cream Sandwiches
- Sparkly Mint Orangeade

Garden Patch Party

Our Twig-fenced Garden

Summer brings to the mountains a luxurious harvest of fresh produce, flowers, and friends with appetites. No one will even think of missing your Garden Patch Party, with fabulous summertime food, an irresistible setting, and all the folks who love to love a party.

We begin at Bear Creek with hay bales and big yellow sunflowers alongside wheelbarrows loaded with iced drinks. Your setting can be localized and just as rustic with split-rail fences by a pond or hunks of logs among the trees. Add irresistible fresh foods in lavish abundance, all from the bounty of summer, for a party that will start itself.

With so much available to work with, add your favorite recipes to ours for a garden patch table of endless variety. Lots of tomatoes? Fry some, slice some, stuff some, chop some – all on the same menu. Awash in watermelon? Cut some small slices for the dainty, chunk the rest and pile it on ice for the hearty. Got corn on the cob? Forget boiling pots of water – grill it alongside kabobs of peppers, cherry tomatoes, onions, and all your own favorites. Crowd getting thirsty? Fill big, frosty sugar-rimmed glasses with limeade and lemonade. Fancy some fruit? You can't beat big bowls of strawberries, some stem-on fresh, some sliced and sugared and piled on shortbread, some – most decadent of all – dipped in chocolate and drizzled with almond bark. Add Colorado peaches, sliced and mixed with berries or sprinkled with lemon juice, and your fruit-lovers will satiate their own desires.

Earth is here so kind, that just tickle her with a hoe and she laughs with a harvest.

Douglas William Jerrold, 1803-1857

Tropical Fruit Salsa

1 cup chopped papaya or mango
1 cup chopped fresh pineapple
½ cup slivered red onion
¼ cup slivered red, orange sweet pepper
3 tablespoons snipped, fresh cilantro
1 teaspoon grated lemon or lime peel
2 tablespoons lemon or lime juice
1 teaspoon grated fresh ginger (optional)

In a medium bowl, stir together all ingredients.

Cover and chill for 8-24 hours. Makes about 18 small servings.

Fried Green Tomatoes

3 tablespoons unbleached all-purpose flour
½ cup cornmeal
1 teaspoon kosher salt
1 teaspoon freshly ground black pepper
½ cup canola oil
4 large green tomatoes, cut into ½-inch slices

In a shallow bowl, mix together the flour, cornmeal, salt, and pepper.

In a large sauté pan, heat the canola oil over medium heat until hot, but not smoking.

Dredge the tomato slices in the cornmeal mixture.

Fry in the oil until golden brown, 3 to 5 minutes per side.

Remove with a slotted spatula and drain on paper towels briefly. Serve hot.

Tropical Fruit Salsa

Garden Patch Party

Spiked Watermelon

1 bottle (750 ml) vodka
(I suggest a mid-range vodka.)

One 10-pound or larger chilled, whole watermelon with seeds (Seedless won't work.)

Cut a plug from the watermelon about 2 inches deep and the shape of the bottle opening. (I held the cap against the melon and traced it with the knife to get the exact size the cut should be.)

Save the plug that you cut out.

Turn the bottle (carefully and slowly) upside down and stick it into the melon. Push it down tightly against the melon. Let it drain in for a couple of hours or until most of the vodka has been absorbed into the watermelon.

If your melon takes the vodka fairly fast, you can push the plug back in. Also do this if you want to transport it.

Refrigerate for a few hours. Slice and serve. If not eaten in 2 days, the melon will become very mushy.

Variation: Minty Spiked Watermelon

1 cup sugar
2 tablespoons lemon juice
1 (750 ml) bottle vodka
2 fresh mint sprigs
1 whole watermelon, 10 pounds or larger

Dissolve the sugar in the lemon juice. Pour out ¼ cup vodka and add the lemon mixture and the mint sprigs to the bottle. Cap, shake, and let sit from 1 hour to overnight for the flavors to develop. Fill the melon as described above.

Grilled Lemon Pepper Chicken

4 6-8 ounce boneless chicken breasts
¼ cup lemon juice
¼ cup olive oil
2 teaspoons Lemon Pepper Seasoning Mix

Mix together the juice, oil, and seasoning mix. Marinate the chicken in the mix for at least an hour. Grill or broil for 4 minutes on each side, or until done.

Cone Fruit Trees

These are decorative and tasty.
Create your own fruit forest for a crowd from the following simple ingredients.

Styrofoam cones of varying sizes from 10 inches to 16 inches (available at your local craft store)

Green, leafy lettuce

Colored toothpicks

Assorted fruit such as melon balls, firm berries, pineapple chunks, cherries, kiwi chunks

Wrap leafy lettuce around each cone, completely concealing the styrofoam. Secure with small toothpicks or a craft-size staple gun.

Cover each tree with fruit, using the colored toothpicks as spears. Leave enough of the toothpick exposed to grasp and remove the fruit for eating.

Serve with yogurt as a dip.

Ice Cream Sandwiches

Best Oatmeal Cookies *(page 57)*
Ice Cream

For the perfect summer treat, make ice cream sandwiches with our Best Oatmeal Cookies and your favorite ice cream.

Just spread the softened ice cream on a cookie, top with another, and freeze.

Thaw at room temperature for 20 minutes before serving on a pretty tray.

Note: Use a quality hard-packed ice cream.

Last night, there came a frost,
which has done great damage to my garden...
It is sad that Nature will play such tricks
on us poor mortals,
inviting us with sunny smiles to confide in her,
and then, when we are entirely within her power,
striking us to the heart.

Nathaniel Hawthorne, 1804-1864

Menu

Tropical Fruit Salsa
Grilled Lemon Chicken
Fried Green Tomatoes
Spiked Watermelon
Cone Fruit Tree
Ice Cream Sandwiches
Sparkly Mint Orangeade

Sparkly Mint Orangeade

½ cup fresh mint
1 cup orange juice
(fresh or concentrate)
1 cup lemonade
(fresh or concentrate)
1-liter bottle club soda
(If you like it a bit sweeter, substitute tonic water.)

In a pitcher combine ½ the mint (hold back about 10 leaves for garnishing glasses), orange juice, lemonade and tonic water. "Muddle" the mint to release the oils.

Strain the mixture, pressing liquid from mint leaves. Stir in club soda. Garnish with 10 mint leaves.

Easily doubled for a larger gathering.

Okay, so this was so not expected!
My boyfriend decides that we
are running away for a night and here we are!
This was the perfect setting –
a cozy cottage, a small fire, and a poem from my love
and then he was on his knees asking the question
I have waited a lifetime to hear
and I said "Yes!"
We will definitely be back!
This was the best weekend of my life
and one I will never forget!
Oh gosh, how do I tell my mom?
Tomorrow is April Fool's!

– guest journal

Picnic for Just Two

- Grilled Chicken
- Glazed Pineapple-Zucchini Bread
- Caprese Sandwiches
- Albino Gazpacho
- The Best Oatmeal Cookies
- Aguas Frescas

Picnic for Just Two

A picnic evokes feelings of leisure, relaxation and fun. It can be a romantic adventure, a family celebration or just an excuse to break from the routine. My most memorable picnic was an evening cookout at Lake Michigan with my family when I was a teenager. We grilled steaks, buried corn on the cob in the hot coals, and roasted marshmallows for s'mores for dessert. We kids ate our steaks with our fingers and it is still the best steak I have ever had.

Picnics in the foothills of the Rocky Mountains offer fantastic vistas, creeks to sit by and crisp mountain air. Our sparkling waters of Evergreen Lake, with paddle-boats, sailboats and canoes, make a floating picnic more than fun. To our "Picnic For Just Two" add a bottle of your favorite wine or our "aguas frescas," fresh and light. Breathe the mountain air, adore the mountain scenery, and love the one you're with. You may even want to cut your steaks and eat them with your fingers!

After snowshoeing up Chief Mountain,
and getting engaged during a picnic lunch
at the top, we returned for a peaceful and romantic
evening in the Evergreen Suite.
Nothing could have been more perfect.

- guest journal

*Seating themselves on the green sward,
they eat while the corks fly and there is talk, laughter and merriment, and
perfect freedom, for the universe is their drawing room and the sun their lamp.
Besides, they have appetite, nature's gift, which lends to such a meal
a vivacity unknown indoors, however beautiful the surroundings.*

Jean Anthelme Brillat-Savarin, 1755-1826

Glazed Pineapple-Zucchini Bread

Bread

1 cup brown sugar
½ cup unsalted butter
1 cup shredded zucchini
1 cup canned crushed pineapple
2 eggs
2 cups flour
1 teaspoon baking soda
1 teaspoon cinnamon
¼ teaspoon allspice
¼ teaspoon salt
½ cup chopped walnuts

Glaze

½ cup powdered sugar
1 tablespoon pineapple juice
1 teaspoon corn syrup
¼ teaspoon cinnamon

Preheat oven to 350°. Grease and lightly flour the bottom of a 9x5-inch loaf pan. In a large bowl, cream the brown sugar and butter until light and fluffy. Stir in zucchini, pineapple, and eggs. Add flour, baking soda, cinnamon, allspice, and salt; blend well. Fold in walnuts. Spread the batter into the prepared pan. Bake for 60-70 minutes. Cool for 10 minutes and remove from pan. Combine all glaze ingredients in a small bowl, mixing till smooth. Spoon over the top of the warm bread.

Picnic Recipes

A picnic is more than a meal; it's a pleasurable state of mind.

A Picnic for Just Two
is entertaining you can do ahead of
time, with no last-minute stress,
as everything is pre-prepared.
Add a bottle of your favorite wine and
find the best scenery you can.
Just serve at your convenience when
hunger strikes and when you have
arrived at your ideal location.

For protein,
grill fresh chicken pieces
and serve cold,
seasoned with salt and pepper.
Even better,
chunk it into bite-size
pieces and grill on a skewer
for picnic finger food.

Caprese Sandwich

2 crusty baguettes or 2 large crusty rolls or
4 slices focaccia bread
¼ cup olive oil
⅓ cup fresh whole basil leaves
4 small ripe fresh tomatoes–use yellow also if available
6 ounces wet or buffalo mozzarella cheese, thinly sliced
sliced kalamata olives (optional)
salt and fresh ground pepper to taste

Cut bread in half. Layer sliced tomatoes and sliced cheese and olives on one half. Layer basil over all. Drizzle with olive oil, season with salt and pepper, and top with the other half.

Albino Gazpacho

3 cucumbers
1 clove garlic
3 cups chicken broth
2 cups sour cream
1 cup plain yogurt
3 tablespoons white vinegar
2 teaspoons salt
2 teaspoons pepper

Puree cucumber and garlic in blender. Mix with all ingredients and serve cold. Garnish with diced tomato, fresh parsley, or scallions.

The Best Oatmeal Cookies

1 cup butter, softened
1 cup firmly packed brown sugar
½ cup granulated sugar
2 eggs
1 teaspoon vanilla
1 tablespoon crushed pineapple
1½ cups flour
1 teaspoon baking soda
1 teaspoon cinnamon
½ teaspoon salt
3 cups quick oats
1 cup raisins
1 cup chocolate chips
½ cup walnuts

Heat oven to 350°.

Beat together butter and sugars until creamy. Add eggs, vanilla and pineapple; beat well. Add combined flour, baking soda, cinnamon and salt; mix well. Stir in oats, raisins, chocolate chips and walnuts; mix well. Drop spoonfuls on cookie sheet.

Bake 10-12 minutes or until golden brown. Cool 1 minute on cookie sheet; remove to wire rack.

Note: For ice cream sandwiches, I make small cookies. See page 51 for directions.

When we should live together in a cozy little cot,
Hid in a nest of roses, with a fairy garden-spot,
Where the vines were ever fruited and the weather ever fine,
And the birds were ever singing for that old sweetheart of mine...

James Whitcomb Riley, 1849-1916

Menu

Grilled Chicken
Glazed Pineapple-Zucchini Bread
Caprese Sandwiches
Albino Gazpacho
The Best Oatmeal Cookies
Aguas Frescas

Aguas Frescas

1 cup ripe melon, diced
cantaloupe, honeydew or watermelon
5 cups water
2 teaspoons honey
¼ cup sugar
¼ cup diced fruit

Purée fruit, water, honey and sugar in a blender. Place a small amount of diced fruit in each glass and add the Aguas Frescas.

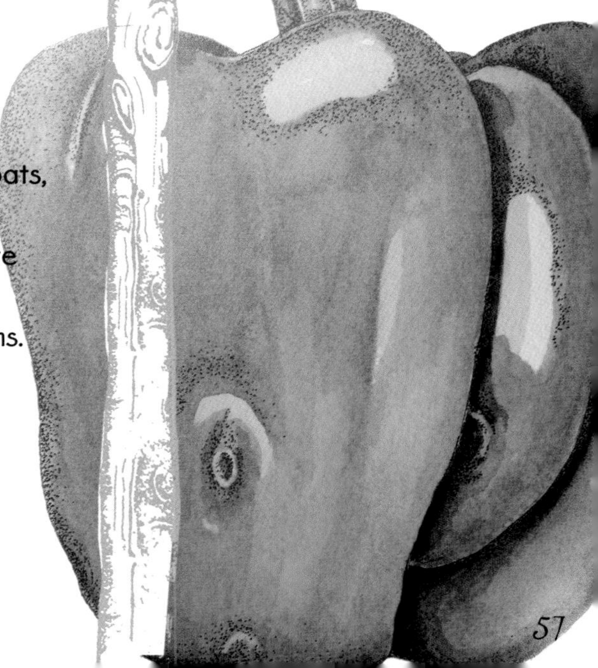

More Summer Recipes

Plum Galette

1 sheet of puff pastry
1 tablespoon flour
½ cup finely ground hazelnuts or walnuts
2 tablespoons light brown sugar
1 tablespoon cornstarch
1 teaspoon salt
5 plums, sliced into ½-inch-thick wedges
3 tablespoons granulated sugar
1 large egg, lightly beaten
Plum jam

Preheat oven to 425° with rack in lower third.

On a lightly floured surface, roll out pastry to 16x18-inch rectangle. Transfer to baking sheet.

In a small bowl, combine flour, hazelnuts, brown sugar, cornstarch and salt; spread to cover middle of dough, leaving a 3-inch border all around.

Arrange plums in rows, slightly overlapping each other and alternating direction of each row.

Sprinkle plums with granulated sugar. Fold dough to enclose edges; brush dough with egg wash.

Chill 30 minutes in refrigerator.

Bake 10 minutes. Reduce oven heat to 400°; bake until pastry is golden brown and plums are softened, about 30 minutes – let cool to room temperature.

Heat jam in a small saucepan over low heat – let cool slightly and brush over plum slices and serve warm.

You may substitute apples or pears for the plums.

Rhubarb Bread

1½ cups brown sugar
1 egg
⅔ cup oil
1 cup buttermilk
1 teaspoon soda
2½ cups flour
1 teaspoon vanilla
¼ teaspoon salt
1½ cups chopped raw rhubarb

Mix all ingredients in bowl except rhubarb. Beat with mixer for 3 minutes. Fold in rhubarb until combined.

Grease and flour two standard size loaf pans.

Pour batter into pans and bake at 325° for 60 minutes.

Rhubarb Squares

½ cup oil
2 cups sugar
1 egg
1 teaspoon vanilla
1 cup sour milk
2 cups flour
1 teaspoon salt
1 teaspoon baking soda
2 cups chopped rhubarb

Mix oil, sugar and egg well.

Add vanilla and milk.

Stir in flour, salt and baking soda. Mix well - but don't over-mix.

Add rhubarb, stir in just until combined.

Pour into a greased 9x13-inch baking pan.

Bake at 325° for 40-50 minutes.

Fruit Tart

12 ounces cream cheese
3½ tablespoons powdered sugar
3 tablespoons milk
1 purchased sponge cake tart base
Cut fruits

Mix cream cheese, sugar and milk into a creamy spreadable mixture with electric hand mixer.

Spread carefully and evenly over tart. Top with cut fruits such as strawberries, blueberries, grapes, kiwi, or raspberries. (Melons, bananas, and apples do not work well.)

The breakfast was fantastic.
All your smiles made your inn feel like family.
Next visit we want to help in the kitchen, OK?
- guest journal

Baked Orange Pecan French Toast

4 eggs
⅔ cup orange juice
⅓ cup milk
¼ cup sugar
½ teaspoon vanilla
¼ teaspoon nutmeg
8 pieces of Texas-style toast cut diagonally
½ cup chopped pecans

Beat together eggs, juice, milk, sugar, vanilla and nutmeg.

Arrange bread in large baking dish (be sure to spray generously with non-stick oil) with bread filling the surface of dish. You may need to get creative in making triangles fill the space nicely; cut smaller triangles if needed.

Top with egg mixture. Refrigerate 2 hours, up to overnight; the liquid will be absorbed.

Bake at 350° for 20 minutes.

Sprinkle with pecans and bake for 10 minutes more.

Serve with Orange Syrup.

Orange Syrup

½ cup sugar
½ cup butter
1 cup orange juice

Combine and cook over low heat.

Do not boil.

Home-baked bread is
the ultimate comfort food.
Everyone has
a personal favorite,
and bread is the foundation of
many of the Inn's best recipes.
It's crusty or soft,
it's yeasty or sweet...
mmm, bread!

Anne's Banana Bread

3-4 very ripe bananas
2 cups sugar
1 teaspoon baking soda
¼ teaspoon salt
4 eggs
4 cups flour
½ cup vegetable oil
1 cup buttermilk

In a large bowl combine the bananas, sugar, baking soda and salt. Blend with elecric mixer at medium speed, about one minute.

Add eggs one at a time, blending thoroughly after each addition. Mix in flour, oil and buttermilk and beat 2 minutes or until smooth and well blended.

Pour batter into 2 well-greased 9x5x3-inch loaf pans. Bake in a 350° oven on center rack for 60 minutes.

Strawberry Bread

1½ cup flour
1 cup sugar
1½ teaspoon cinnamon
½ teaspoon salt
½ teaspoon baking soda
2 eggs, beaten
½ cup oil
1 cup fresh strawberries, or frozen ones drained

Mix together flour, sugar, cinnamon, salt and soda.

Combine eggs, oil and strawberries. Add to dry ingredients. Pour into a greased and floured 9x5-inch loaf pan. Bake 50-60 minutes in a 350° oven.

Serve with Strawberry Butter.

Strawberry Butter

1 10-ounce package of frozen strawberries
1 cup soft butter
1 cup sifted powdered sugar

Combine ingredients in blender.

With due respect to the authentic English Trifle, we believe you will find this variation very simple, quick, and dressed to impress! Our Heavenly Breakfast Trifle is not only scrumptious, but also healthful and light.

This delicious concoction has won its way into our hearts; we love to prepare it, and our guests love to partake. We have used these recipes (there's another in our Winter "More Recipes" pages) with variations all through the year for breakfasts, teas, and luncheons. They are adaptable, easy and so satisfying. Presentation here is such an important ingredient. For any trifle you will want a clear glass bowl so the layers of yum are visible.

Heavenly Breakfast Trifle

1 angel food cake, home-made or purchased, torn into bite-sized pieces
1 32-ounce container of vanilla low-fat yogurt
1 pint fresh strawberries, cleaned and sliced
1 large banana, sliced
1 pint blueberries (or other berries)
1 cup granola of your choice (we make our own and add dried fruit)

Layer in your glass bowl half the angel food cake pieces.

Spread half of the yogurt.

Layer half of the fruit assortment.

Layer half of the granola.

Repeat layering, reserving a few berries to garnish the top.

Note: Our signature trifle recipe is on page 25.

Lynda's Sassy Salsa

½ pound tomatillos
½ pound plum tomatoes
1 medium onion
5 Anaheim peppers
6 limes
1 bunch cilantro
a pinch of kosher salt
4 jalapeno peppers (optional)

Remove skins and clean tomatillos; cut in half. Cut plum tomatoes into quarters. Peel and cut onion into quarters. Remove stems from peppers. Place all in food processor with the juice of 6 limes, cilantro, and salt.

Strawberry Coffee Cake

1 cup all-purpose flour
½ cup sugar
2 teaspoons baking powder
1 egg
½ cup milk
2 tablespoons butter or margarine, melted
1½ cups sliced fresh strawberries

Topping
½ cup flour
½ cup sugar
¼ cup cold butter
¼ cup chopped pecans (optional)

In a large bowl, combine the dry ingredients. In another bowl, combine the egg, milk, and butter; stir into dry ingredients just until moistened. Pour into a greased 8-inch round baking dish. Top with sliced strawberries.

For topping, combine flour and sugar in a small bowl; cut in butter until crumbly. Stir in pecans if desired; sprinkle over strawberries. Bake at 375° for 30-35 minutes or until a toothpick inserted near the center comes out clean. Cut into squares; serve warm.

Note: You may "dress this up" any way you like; bake in a heart-shaped pan or your favorite pan. For presentation add a few fresh strawberries and pansies.

Raspberry Bread Pudding

2 cups milk
½ cup sugar
3 eggs beaten lightly
¼ teaspoon nutmeg
½ teaspoon vanilla
3 cups French bread
torn into 1-inch pieces
2 cups fresh raspberries
2 tablespoons confectioner's sugar

Preheat oven to 375°.

In a saucepan, bring milk to a boil. Remove from heat and stir in sugar. Cool 10 minutes. Whisk in beaten eggs, nutmeg and vanilla.

Place bread cubes in a buttered 1½ quart baking dish. Spoon 1 cup of berries over the top.

Pour milk and egg mixture over bread and fruit; bake for 1 hour, until set and starting to brown. Test with knife through center. If it comes out clean, the pudding is done. Do not undercook!

To make sauce, blend 1 cup raspberries with 2 tablespoons confectioner's sugar, and strain through a sieve.

When pudding is cool, slice and dust with confectioner's sugar. Drizzle raspberry sauce over the top.

My daughter Roxy and I head to Fern Gulch each early August to harvest the sweet little wild raspberries for our cereal, ice cream and a perfect garnish to this bread pudding.

Roxy's Baked Apple Clafouti

1 cup thinly sliced apples
1 teaspoon cinnamon
2 teaspoons vanilla
½ teaspoon nutmeg
2 tablespoons lemon juice
1 cup flour
4 tablespoons sugar
½ cup whole milk
2 eggs
2 teaspoons baking powder
½ teaspoon salt
2 tablespoons melted butter
¼ stick real butter
⅓ cup chopped nuts

Mix thinly sliced apples, cinnamon, vanilla, nutmeg, lemon juice in bowl and let marinate for 1 hour.

In small bowl, blend flour, sugar, milk, eggs, baking powder, salt and melted butter. Do not over-mix.

Melt ¼ stick butter in 10-inch Pyrex pie pan; swirl around to cover edges of pie pan. Place nuts and apple mixture into pie pan.

Add the batter.

Bake at 350° for 30 minutes or until top starts to brown and returns when pushed with finger.
When done go around edges of pie pan with knife and invert onto large platter.

Serve with warm maple syrup.

Note: You'll find other versions of this recipe on pages 34 and 79.

*Good food is elixir for a troubled mind.
Carefully prepared and lovingly served,
good food brings quiet,
contentment, and perspective.*

Apple Pie Compote

7 Red and/or Golden Delicious apples
3 Macintosh apples
1 cup raisins
⅓ cup sugar
2 tablespoons lemon juice
1 teaspoon cinnamon
1 teaspoon nutmeg
1 teaspoon allspice
10 whole cloves
¼ cup water

Core and chop apples into chucks.

Combine all ingredients in 4-6 quart pot.

Simmer until apples are soft, stirring occasionally, approximately 40 minutes.

Remove cloves.

Serve in dessert stems or champagne glasses with dollop of freshly whipped cream.

Raspberry Cream Cheese

Use this as a dip for apple slices or a sweet colorful spread for bagels or muffins.

In a food processor, or in a bowl with a fork, blend 8 ounces soft cream cheese, ¾ cup thawed and drained frozen raspberries (or fresh), 2 tablespoons honey and 1 tablespoon lemon juice until smooth.

Serve immediately or store covered for up to one week.

Makes 1 cup.

I use wild little raspberries I collect from our Fern Gulch and around the Inn. Home-grown are always the best, but fresh from your market are wonderful, too!

Autumn

'Tis a gift to be simple
'Tis a gift to be free
'Tis a gift to come down where we ought to be
And when we find ourselves in the place that's right
'twill be in the valley of love and delight.

Shaker hymn, "Simple Gifts"

Autumn at the Inn

They's something kindo' harty-like about the atmusfere
When the heat of summer's over and the coolin' fall is here -
Of course we miss the flowers, and the blossums on the trees,
And the mumble of the hummin'-birds and buzzin' of the bees;
But the air's so appetizin'; and the landscape through the haze
Of a crisp and sunny morning of the airly autumn days
Is a pictur' that no painter has the colorin' to mock -
When the frost is on the punkin and the fodder's in the shock.

James Whitcomb Riley, 1849-1916

There is such a sweet, midwestern simplicity to the works of James Whitcomb Riley.
Coming from his ancestory, I warm to the bone when I read his Indiana writings.
I have a large collection of antique poetry books and among them are all I can find of James Whitcomb Riley.

Poultry and My Past

Autumn Brunch

- Breakfast Granola
- Baked Oatmeal
- Baked Apple Gala
- Miriam's Eggs Eisenhower
- Karin's Ramos Fizz Cocktail

Poultry & My Past

Aunt Ginny as a child with her Henrietta

Poultry played a part in my childhood with my father's 20,000 turkeys, Grandpa's income from eggs, and my sister and I modeling for photographs with Tom Turkey…but shopping for chickens from a catalog was a new experience in my life as an innkeeper! When twenty-five chicks were delivered in a small box, we were off on a laughable and educational odyssey. My husband still contends that each egg is worth about five bucks.

The chicks progressed from life in a child's swimming pool to their first "coop home," and through sad experiences with golden retrievers and a neighboring fox. But some survived and more were purchased, so finally they began to produce eggs for the inn.

Occasionally, children are guests, and when one of them collects eggs and experiences that "farm feeling," for the first time, the moment is priceless. One cutie, touching the warm eggs and fascinated by the busy hens, asked me earnestly, "Where's the farmer?"

Though our rooster, "The Donald," is no longer with us these days, his career cut short by early morning noise, we do have all the eggs we need, compliments of "The Girls," Henrietta, Goldie, Lacey and their many chic-chick friends among the Silver-Laced Wyandottes, White Rocks, and Rhode Island Reds.

With all this accessibility to our own farm-fresh eggs, brunch at the Highland Haven is a very 'eggy' matter. Guests can feast on Miriam's Eggs Eisenhower with their choice of three yummy breakfast meats, sweet rolls or coffee cake, and the freshest fruits of the season. We bring out the eggs again for our wonderful nutmeg-sprinkled Karin's Ramos Fizz Cocktail, and nobody turns it down!

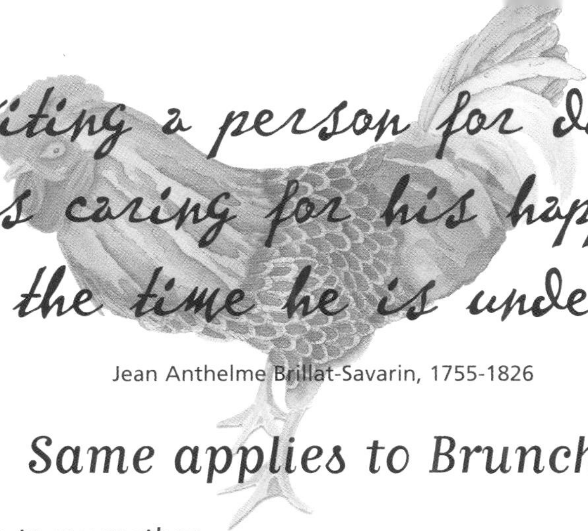

Inviting a person for dinner means caring for his happiness throughout the time he is under your roof.

Jean Anthelme Brillat-Savarin, 1755-1826

Same applies to Brunch!

Here is a note from my cousin Adam to my mother, when we started raising our own chickens.

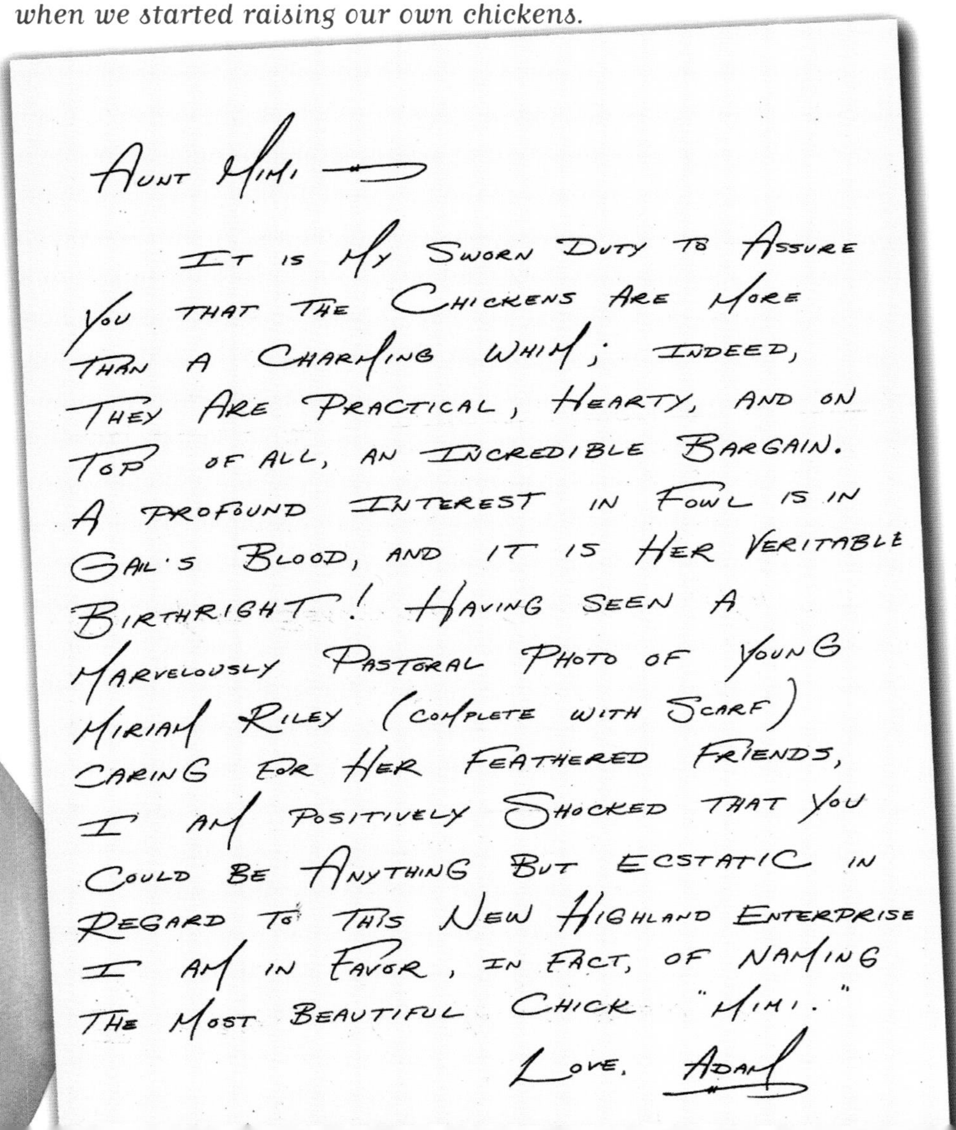

AUNT MIMI —

IT IS MY SWORN DUTY TO ASSURE YOU THAT THE CHICKENS ARE MORE THAN A CHARMING WHIM; INDEED, THEY ARE PRACTICAL, HEARTY, AND ON TOP OF ALL, AN INCREDIBLE BARGAIN. A PROFOUND INTEREST IN FOWL IS IN GAIL'S BLOOD, AND IT IS HER VERITABLE BIRTHRIGHT! HAVING SEEN A MARVELOUSLY PASTORAL PHOTO OF YOUNG MIRIAM RILEY (COMPLETE WITH SCARF) CARING FOR HER FEATHERED FRIENDS, I AM POSITIVELY SHOCKED THAT YOU COULD BE ANYTHING BUT ECSTATIC IN REGARD TO THIS NEW HIGHLAND ENTERPRISE I AM IN FAVOR, IN FACT, OF NAMING THE MOST BEAUTIFUL CHICK "MIMI."

LOVE, ADAM

Gail with Mom, Mimi

Autumn Brunch

In the fall, Baked Oatmeal or Breakfast Granola will cozy up the kitchen with fragrance and warm those tummies with comfort food to please the choosiest palate. For a moveable feast, we load up cheery gift bags with our crunchy granola, brighten them up for guests and other friends, and run fall right into winter with these pretty, tasty presents.

Breakfast Granola

5 cups uncooked oats
1 cup sliced almonds
1 cup sesame seeds
1 cup wheat germ
1 cup sunflower seeds
1 cup safflower oil
1 cup honey
1 cup raisins

Preheat oven to 325°.

Combine dry ingredients in bowl and mix well.

Heat oil and honey together in small pan until melted.

Pour over dry ingredients and mix well.

Spread mixture onto cookie sheets and bake for approximately 20 minutes. When cool, add raisins.

Store granola in an airtight container to keep it crunchy.

Baked Oatmeal

3 cups of quick oats
1 cup brown sugar
2 teaspoons baking powder
1 teaspoon cinnamon
1 teaspoon salt
1 cup milk
½ cup butter melted
2 eggs beaten
1 teaspoon vanilla

Combine oats, sugar, baking powder, cinnamon and salt in large mixing bowl.

In small bowl combine milk, butter, beaten eggs & vanilla.

Add milk mixture to dry ingredients and mix well.

Pour into 9x13-inch baking dish and bake for 40-45 minutes at 350°.

Be creative here - add apples, raisins or berries if you like. Smells wonderful while baking.

Baked Apple Gala

8 crisp Gala apples
4 tablespoons sugar
4 tablespoons brown sugar
1 teaspoon cinnamon
8 large pieces of lemon peel
3 tablespoons softened butter
1 tablespoon dried cherries
1 vanilla bean
4 cinnamon sticks

Preheat oven to 375°.

Remove bottoms of apples, and core. Butter a large glass or porcelain dish and sprinkle with 2 tablespoons of sugar. Arrange the apples upright in the dish.

Fill the center of each apple with 1 teaspoon of brown sugar, ⅛ teaspoon of cinnamon and 1 piece of lemon peel. Rub the top of each apple with ¼ tablespoon soft butter and sprinkle with more sugar.

Sprinkle the dried cherries around the apples and add the vanilla bean and cinnamon sticks to the dish.

Bake for 35-45 minutes.

Miriam's Eggs Eisenhower

- 4 tablespoons butter
- 5 tablespoons all-purpose flour
- 2 cups milk
- Salt and pepper to taste
- 1 cup saltine cracker crumbs
- 1 cup grated cheddar cheese
- ½ of a 2 ounce jar of chopped pimentos
- 8 hard boiled eggs, peeled & chopped

Butter an 8-inch baking dish and preheat the oven to 350°.

Melt the butter over medium heat in a heavy saucepan.

Stir in the flour and cook, stirring constantly, until the mixture thickens, about two minutes. Add the milk, continuing to stir as sauce thickens.

Add the salt and pepper, lower the heat and cook for 2-3 minutes more. Remove from heat.

Sprinkle half of the cracker crumbs on the prepared dish. Pour half of white sauce over the crumbs. Sprinkle with half of the cheese, pimentos and chopped eggs. Repeat layers ending with white sauce sprinkled with cheese and cracker crumbs.

Bake for 30-40 minutes until bubbly. Do not overbake; you are really just re-heating your ingredients.

Menu

Breakfast Granola
Baked Oatmeal
Baked Apple Gala
Miriam's Eggs Eisenhower
Karin's Ramos Fizz Cocktail

Karin's Ramos Fizz Cocktail

This drink makes a brunch so very festive!

Mix in blender for one batch:

1 small can limeade from frozen concentrate
1 small can lemonade from frozen concentrate
3 egg whites
1/3 full ice cubes
1 small can gin
1 small can half and half

Blend until frothy. Pour into your prettiest glasses and sprinkle with nutmeg.

Gail with Mom, Gramma and Great-Gramma

As I awoke to the crisp fall air –
I've come to rediscover the beauty
and tranquility that is Colorado.

- guest journal

Wild West Dinner Party

- Baked Golden Trout
- Smashed Yukan Gold Potatoes
- Garden Fresh Stuffing
- Marinated Mushrooms
- French Style Green Beans
- Apple Clafouti

Wild West

My Little Partner Jaxon

Ah, the wild, wild west! Long ago, where the High Plains meet the Rocky Mountains, a hardy assortment of mountain men, scouts, and pioneers established a tradition of living off the land. With what comforts they could find or create, with what foods they could hunt, grow, or reap from nature, they made a life for themselves and their kin in a land that was wild in every way.

Here in the mountains near old Evergreen, we have restored the vintage Dailey Cabin, built in 1884 and reputed to be the oldest log cabin in the valley. John Dailey, a founder of Denver's Rocky Mountain News, loved to travel with friends to Evergreen's Bear Creek Valley, where he built his cabin of hand-hewn logs. We have lovingly refurbished this sturdy steep-roofed timbered building for our western gatherings and for the serving of our mountain cuisine. Memories of Dailey's 19th-century life on his forays into his beloved mountains still fill our cabin, in the original stone fireplace, the many vintage photographs, and the hand-crafted and antique furniture. The sounds and scents of the creek and the valley speak to us as they did to him.

Now the rugged land and lifestyle of those early folks and their mountain settings call out to us, and all the guests at your Wild West Party will respond eagerly to that call. Lacking an old mountain cabin need not cramp your party style. Each area of the country had its own pioneers, and your décor will come from your ancestors' experiences: prairie schooners, gold rush tents, high plains soddies, and lonely dugouts housed the hardy ones who peopled this land's beginnings. Western décor is so appealing with calico and denim, red neckerchiefs

Standing alone on the mountaintop it is easy to realize
that whatever special nests we make -
leaves and moss like the marmots and birds,
or tents or piled stone -
we all dwell in a house of one room...

John, Viscount Morley of Blackburn, 1838-1923

and leather, rustic candles, dried natural arrangements, and even, on the plains, the tumbling tumbleweeds of story and song.

Dads and Grandpas will like this gathering, especially when it's done in their honor on Father's Day or Grandparents' Day. Decorate with old photos of the guest of honor, and choose one of them to enlarge in sepia tones for invitations, party favors, and other mementos. In advance, find a few guests who can provide stories of Grandpa's past, and hope that he'll add a few of his own.

For those who imbibe, begin with a short "neat" glass of Scotch or bourbon or a rich red wine. For those who don't, offer cranberry juice on the rocks with a chunk of lime, or cold, spicy apple cider. Add rustic trays of appetizers and a western storyteller or humorous cowboy poet who may, just for fun, begin a tale before your trout or steak dinner and finish it with Apple Clafouti.

Most of all, focus on the friendships and kinships that thrived in the West, where the building of a life was so demanding that neighbors and families depended heavily upon one another. There, in our own time, a country spirit of helpfulness survives in the towns and villages founded upon 19th-century vision and determination.

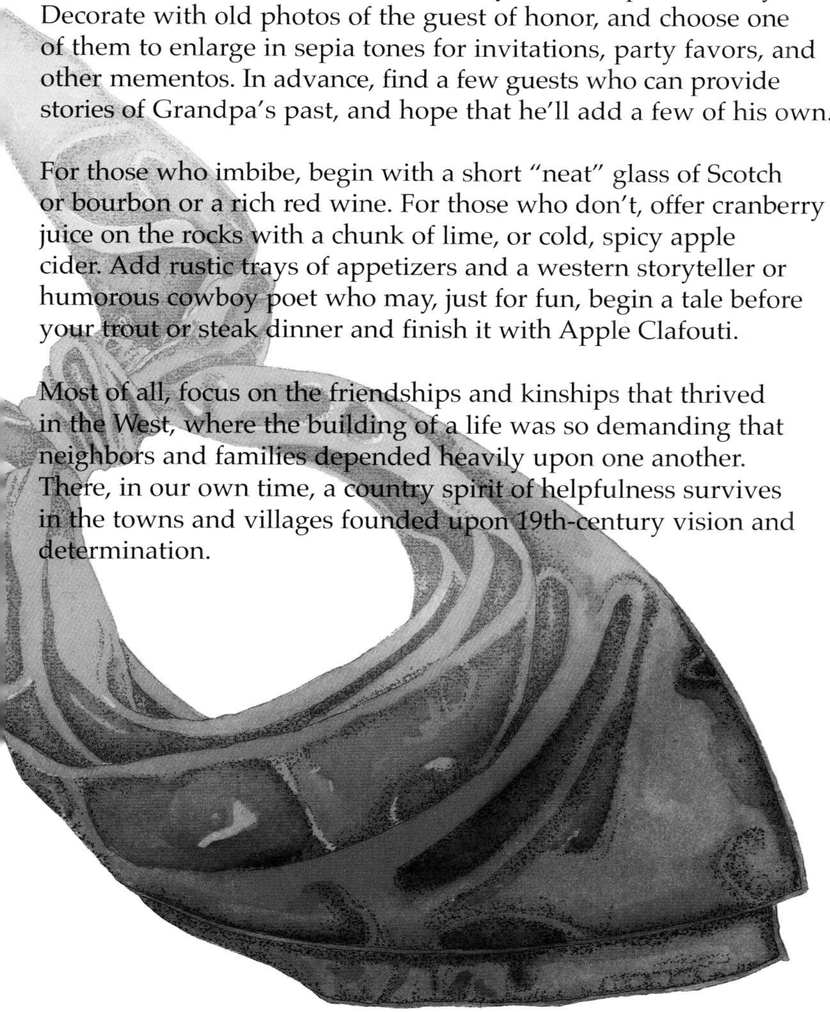

Grandpa Floyd with Baby Mimi, my Mom

Wild West Dinner Party

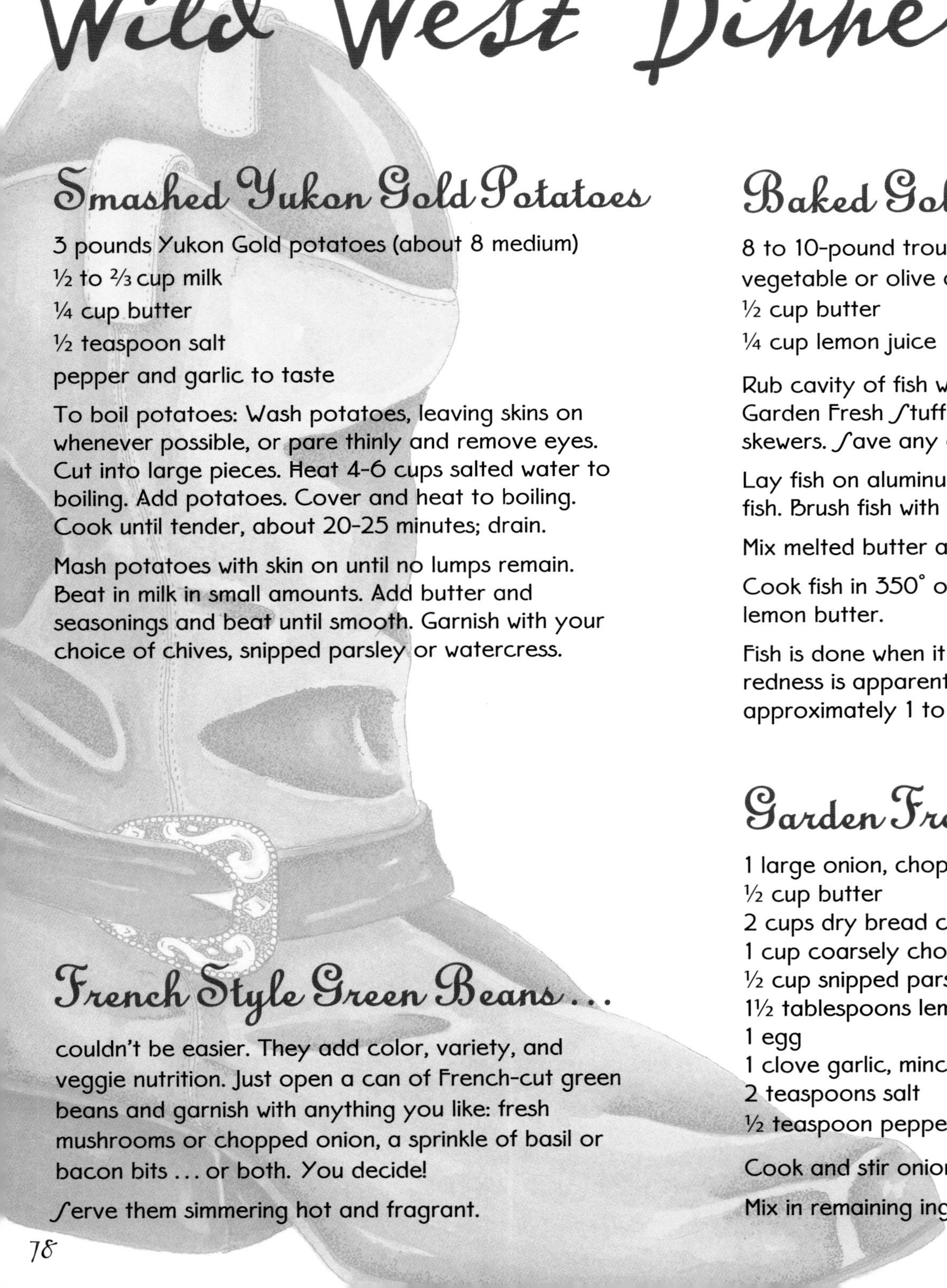

Smashed Yukon Gold Potatoes

3 pounds Yukon Gold potatoes (about 8 medium)
½ to ⅔ cup milk
¼ cup butter
½ teaspoon salt
pepper and garlic to taste

To boil potatoes: Wash potatoes, leaving skins on whenever possible, or pare thinly and remove eyes. Cut into large pieces. Heat 4-6 cups salted water to boiling. Add potatoes. Cover and heat to boiling. Cook until tender, about 20-25 minutes; drain.

Mash potatoes with skin on until no lumps remain. Beat in milk in small amounts. Add butter and seasonings and beat until smooth. Garnish with your choice of chives, snipped parsley or watercress.

French Style Green Beans . . .

couldn't be easier. They add color, variety, and veggie nutrition. Just open a can of French-cut green beans and garnish with anything you like: fresh mushrooms or chopped onion, a sprinkle of basil or bacon bits . . . or both. You decide!

Serve them simmering hot and fragrant.

Baked Golden Trout

8 to 10-pound trout
vegetable or olive oil
½ cup butter
¼ cup lemon juice

Rub cavity of fish with salt and pepper. Stuff with Garden Fresh Stuffing (optional). Close opening with skewers. Save any extra stuffing in a small baking dish.

Lay fish on aluminum foil large enough to enclose fish. Brush fish with oil. Place in shallow roasting pan.

Mix melted butter and lemon juice.

Cook fish in 350° oven, brushing occasionally with lemon butter.

Fish is done when it flakes easily with fork and no redness is apparent in meatiest part of fish, approximately 1 to 1½ hours. Serves 10-12.

Garden Fresh Stuffing

1 large onion, chopped
½ cup butter
2 cups dry bread cubes or stuffing
1 cup coarsely chopped carrot
½ cup snipped parsley or dry parsley flakes
1½ tablespoons lemon juice
1 egg
1 clove garlic, minced
2 teaspoons salt
½ teaspoon pepper

Cook and stir onions in butter until clear and tender.

Mix in remaining ingredients and place stuffing into trout.

Apple Clafouti

2 tablespoons unsalted butter
3 red or golden delicious apples, peeled, cored, and cut into ½-inch wedges
¾ cup sugar
¼ teaspoon ground cinnamon
⅔ cup all-purpose flour
4 large eggs
1 cup milk
2 tablespoons calvados or applejack

Heat the butter in an 8-inch skillet. Add the apples, toss to coat. Add half sugar and the cinnamon and cook for approximately 2 minutes to soften the apples. This may be done in advance.

Preheat oven to 400°. Put the remaining sugar, the flour, eggs, milk and Calvados in a blender and process until smooth.

With a slotted spoon, remove the apples from the skillet to a 10-inch round quiche or pie plate, 1½ inches deep. Add the apple liquid to the batter and process just to mix.

Pour batter over apples in pan and place pan on baking sheet. Bake for 40-45 minutes until brown and batter is set. A knife stuck in middle should come out clean if done.

Serve while warm with vanilla bean ice cream. Serves 8-10.

Note: For other versions of this recipe, see pages 34 and 63.

Menu

"Neat" Scotch, Bourbon, Wine, Cranberry Juice

Baked Golden Trout

Smashed Yukon Gold Potatoes

Garden Fresh Stuffing

Marinated Mushrooms *(page 44)*

French Style Green Beans

Apple Clafouti

Vanilla Bean Ice Cream

Rich Coffee

Deer walk upon our mountains, and the quail Whistle about us their spontaneous cries; Sweet berries ripen in the wilderness...

Wallace Stevens, 1879-1923

More Autumn Recipes

Creekside Caramel Apple Bake

¾ cup flour
½ cup sugar
1 teaspoon baking powder
1 teaspoon cinnamon
¼ teaspoon salt
1½ cups peeled and chopped apples
½ cup sliced almonds
½ cup milk

Preheat the oven to 375°.

Grease an 8x8-inch glass baking dish.

In a large bowl combine the flour, sugar, baking powder, cinnamon and salt. Mix well. Add chopped apples and sliced almonds and mix. Add milk and stir well. Spread into baking dish.

Topping
¾ cup brown sugar
¼ cup butter
¾ cup boiling water

In a sauce pan combine sugar, butter, and water.

Stir until butter is melted. Pour the topping over the batter and bake for 1 hour.

Note: Serve with a brunch, but for a great fall dessert simply top with fresh whipped cream.

French Mushroom Soup

½ cup minced onion
1 stick unsalted butter
6 tablespoons all-purpose flour
12 cups chicken stock
2 sprigs parsley
½ bay leaf
1 pinch of thyme
3 pounds mushrooms, trimmed and sliced very thin
½ teaspoon kosher salt
1 teaspoon freshly squeezed lemon juice
4 egg yolks
1 cup heavy cream

In a large stockpot, cook the onion in 4 tablespoons of the butter until soft. Stir in the flour and cook over low heat for 4 minutes without browning. Add the stock, blending it completely with the flour. Add the parsley sprigs, bay leaf, and thyme. Simmer for 20 minutes.

Melt the remaining 4 tablespoons of butter in a large pan. Toss the mushrooms in the butter with salt and lemon juice. Cook 5 minutes. Add the cooked mushrooms to the broth and simmer 5 minutes.

Beat the egg yolks and cream until blended. Stir a cupful of the hot soup into the cream mixture. Add the cream to the soup and heat to below the simmer. If the soup simmers, the yolks will curdle.

Serve immediately, garnished with parsley.

Heavenly Baked Breakfast Pineapple

1 large can of crushed pineapple
2 tablespoons flour
¼ cup sugar
3 eggs beaten
3 slices bread, cubed
3 tablespoons butter
1 tablespoon each sugar & cinnamon, mixed

Lightly grease 9-inch square pan or pie pan.

Mix pineapple, flour and sugar.

Beat eggs and lightly add to the pineapple mixture. Pour into greased pan.

Place bread cubes on top. Melt butter and pour over bread.

Sprinkle with cinnamon and sugar.

Bake at 350° for 45 minutes.

Siblings Joan, Guy, Mom Mimi, Jane and Gail

Autumn Leaf Petite Pastry

The most impressive little morsel of autumn tastiness: Serve for breakfast treat, as cookies, or as dessert with ice cream. Best when served warm.

1 package frozen puff pastry
1 apple
1 egg, whipped for egg wash
4 tablespoons sugar
1 tablespoon ground cloves
1 tablespoon ground cinnamon

Roll out thinly 1 sheet of pastry dough.

Cut out cookies using a leaf for fall, or other favorite shapes for other times. Place pastries on cookie sheets and brush with egg wash.

Core and slice apple in thin strips cut in half.

Mix apples in bowl with sugar, cloves, and cinnamon.

Place spices and two small apple slices on each leaf.

Bake at 400 degrees for about 5 minutes, until rich and brown in color.

Stuffed French Toast

1 loaf of French bread cubed
8 ounces sliced cream cheese
2½ cups milk
8 eggs
1 cup maple syrup
½ teaspoon cinnamon
½ cup melted butter

Spray a 9-inch baking dish with cooking spray.

Layer as follows: bread, sliced cream cheese, bread.

Mix milk, eggs and ½ cup maple syrup. Pour over casserole making sure that bread is saturated.

Sprinkle with cinnamon.

Bake for 2 hours at 350°.

Pour mixture of ½ cup melted butter and ½ cup syrup over all.

Baked Acorn Squash Rings

1 small acorn squash
4 tablespoons unsalted butter cut into small pieces
coarse kosher salt
freshly ground black pepper
⅓ cup packed dark brown sugar

Cut the unpeeled squash crosswise into ½ inch slices and place them on a cutting board. Using a biscuit cutter slightly larger than the seed center, cut out the seeds from each ring and discard.

Place the squash rings on a lightly buttered baking sheet. Dot each ring with butter. Sprinkle with salt and pepper to taste. Sprinkle a bit of brown sugar over each ring.

Bake in a 350° oven for 15 minutes. Turn the rings over, dot with more butter and sugar, and bake until tender, 5 –10 minutes longer. Serve hot.

Vacations mean a change of pace,
a gentleness with ourselves,
a time of rest and renewal,
and a time to stretch ourselves.
The variety expands our spirits:
new lands, new people,
new ways and options.
We owe to ourselves and those
who love us to take vacations.

Classic Bread Pudding

1 loaf French bread
4 cups milk
2 tablespoons vanilla
3 eggs
1½ cups sugar
1 cup raisins

Tear the bread into 1-inch pieces.

Place in large bowl, add milk and vanilla. Mix and cover to let stand at room temperature for one hour.

Mix eggs, sugar and raisins together. Add to milk and bread mixture and stir well.

Pour into buttered casserole dish and bake at 375° for 1 hour.

You may serve warm with whiskey butter sauce over top.

Whiskey Butter Sauce
Melt 4 tablespoons butter in microwave or on stovetop, add ½ cup powdered sugar and 2 tablespoons whiskey, and spoon over the bread pudding.

Gail's Variations on the Classic

Substitute chocolate pieces for raisins.

Substitute fresh raspberries, apples or blueberries for raisins.

Substitute currants, dried cranberries or cherries for raisins.

Note: See page 17 for another version of this recipe.

Ratatouille (ra-ta-tooey)

This family recipe is a perfect complement to meats and fishes.

1 small zucchini cut in ¼ inch rounds
1 small yellow squash cut in ¼ inch rounds
¼ red onion, slice in big chunks
1 large ripe tomato cut in chunks
¼ cup olive oil
1 teaspoon pepper
1 teaspoon garlic salt
¼ cup seasoned breadcrumbs
4 tablespoons Parmesan cheese

In mixing bowl combine the first 7 ingredients, toss gently to cover veggies with oil and spices.

Place in small baking dish.

Sprinkle with breadcrumbs and cheese.

Bake at 350° for 20 minutes.

Sister Jane with Gail and the biggest tom turkey of them all.

Gougéres

5 tablespoons butter
1 teaspoon salt
¼ teaspoon freshly ground pepper
¼ teaspoon freshly ground nutmeg
1 cup water
1 cup all-purpose flour
1 cup grated Gruyère cheese
5 large eggs at room temperature

Add butter, salt, pepper, and nutmeg to 1 cup of water in a medium saucepan and bring to a boil over medium-high heat. When butter melts, reduce heat to low.

Add flour to butter-water mixture all at once and cook over low heat, beating with a wooden spoon for 1 minute, until mixture pulls away from the sides of the pan. Remove from heat.

Add cheese to pan and beat in with a wooden spoon until well incorporated. Add 4 of the eggs, 1 at a time, beating each egg into the batter until thoroughly absorbed. Continue beating mixture until it is smooth, shiny, and firm.

Drop the batter in small spoonfuls onto a lightly greased cookie sheet to form gougéres. Beat remaining egg with ½ tablespoon water, then brush tops of uncooked gougéres with the egg wash.

Bake in upper third of 425° oven for 15-20 minutes or until gougéres are golden and doubled in size. Remove from oven and serve hot, or allow to cool. Makes about 3 dozen gougéres.

Flavored Cream Cheeses

Ideal for breakfast, lunch or brunch! Use low-fat or fat-free cream cheese and experiment with new ingredients. Simply soften the cheese and stir in the enhancement.

Spicy Lemon Chive

8 ounces cream cheese
¾ teaspoon chives, chopped
⅓ teaspoon ground red pepper
1½ tablespoons lemon juice

Honey-Cinnamon

8 ounces cream cheese
1½ tablespoons honey
1 teaspoon cinnamon

Cinnamon-Currant

8 ounces cream cheese
¼ cup currants
1 teaspoon cinnamon
1 tablespoon honey
⅛ teaspoon nutmeg

Orange-Walnut

8 ounces cream cheese
¼ cup minced walnuts
1 tablespoon orange juice

Carrot Cake Breakfast Muffins

1½ cups flour
½ cup whole wheat flour
1¼ cups sugar
1 tablespoon cinnamon
1 teaspoon baking powder
1 teaspoon baking soda
½ teaspoon salt
2 cups finely grated carrot
1 tart apple, finely grated
1 cup golden raisins
1 egg
2 egg whites
½ cup applesauce
¼ cup vegetable oil
1 tablespoon vanilla
2 tablespoons finely chopped nuts
2 tablespoons toasted wheat germ

Preheat oven to 375°.

Spray muffin tin.

Stir together flours, sugar, cinnamon, baking powder, baking soda and salt.

Stir in carrots, apples and raisins.

In another bowl whisk together eggs, apple sauce, oil and vanilla.

Combine wet and dry ingredients until just blended.

Spoon into muffin tins, filling them ¾ full.

Combine nuts and wheat germ; sprinkle over muffin tops.

Bake 15-20 minutes or until tops are golden and springy. Cool briefly in tins and then turn out onto rack. Makes 18 muffins.

Breakfast at the Inn has so many qualities of the past. I call ours "Breakfast in Bread" as so many of our most favorite recipes start with bread. And oftentimes the integrity of the dish relies on the quality and texture of the bread. The sensible act of making use of day-old bread would make all our grammas happy.

In our strata recipe, the better the bread, the better the dish. It is important to have all the bread soaked with your egg mixture so there is no toughness after baking.

In my bread pudding recipes I design the dish around the bread; using cinnamon raisin bagels is one of my favorites. It makes the dish denser and rich tasting. I'll use a French bread for a lighter bread pudding that may include fresh blueberries or cranberries.

Our French toast is one of our hands-down favorites and you can include your favorite ingredients to make it your specialty. Stuff your "Texas toast" (slit opening) with thin slices of apples, pears or cream cheese. Here be sure not to add more liquid than the recipe calls for; it will not soak in and the dish will be too wet.

Gardening at the altitude of 7000 feet has its own unique set of challenges. Thankfully, rhubarb thrives and I can harvest from May through August. My plants are enormous. Did you know that you don't cut but give the stalks a good yank when ripe? This recipe tastes as good as it smells. You will love this.

Strawberry-Rhubarb Betty

1 cup sugar
2 tablespoons flour
¼ teaspoon salt
3 cups fresh strawberries
2 cups thinly sliced fresh rhubarb
4 cups torn pieces of cinnamon or white bread (about 5 slices)
¼ cup melted butter

In large mixing bowl stir together sugar, flour and salt. Add strawberries and rhubarb. Toss until coated.

For topping, place the bread in medium bowl with the melted butter until coated. Transfer half of it to an ungreased casserole or baking dish. Pour the fruit over the bread cubes. Add the remaining bread.

Bake at 375° for 25-30 minutes until bread is lightly browned.

Enjoy while warm. Serves 6.

How blessed I am to be staying here on business!
I've been traveling for the past month and this is my last trip for a while.
What a way to treat myself to pure relaxation.
The sound of the creek, your incredible hospitality, the cozy cottage and beautiful scenery have done wonders for my soul – all in such a short time.

- guest journal

Wintertime

Stand within the swirling mountain snow,
Fluffy soft flakes falling upon your hair
in the windless twilight,
And you will move into a mystic moment in time,
A suspension of self in space, a breath of sudden peace.

Bette Milleson James

Wintertime at the Inn

This trip was an excerpt from a fairy tale.

\- guest journal

Wintertime!

- Snow Bear
- Peanut Butter & Birdseeded Pinecones
- Snow Day
- Minty Cocoa
- Eliza's Homemade Graham Crackers

Snow Bear

Bear Creek Bear

Each year, decorations at the Inn become more and more natural, using simple ideas. Our family favorite is a new twist on an old tradition. When a snow man needs a buddy, bundle up the kids and join efforts to create a new kind of winter creature.

Everyone loves a snow bear.

Simply take a favorite stuffed bear buddy outside to copy . . . the basic method remains the same as for a snow man; just try a bit of "sculpting" to add a fun twist.

Gorgeous Place!
This place will hold special memories for me because I witnessed my first snowfall.
- guest journal

Christmas

and all the winter holidays are just easy to "do." The season has a *spirit* that overtakes all of us, whether we are awash in family traditions or spreading *joy* throughout our homes and communities. Memories of abundant delights in seasons past inspire us to beautiful celebrations old and new. The spirituality of the season, the giving and sharing, the frolicking in the snow – all offer wholesome and rich fun and a veritable treasure chest of memories.

Snow had fallen,
Snow on snow,
Snow on snow...

Christina Rosetti, 1830-1894

The moon above the eastern wood
Shone at its full: the hill range stood
Transfigured in the silver flood,
Its blown snows flashing cold and keen,
Dead white, save where some sharp ravine
Took shadow, or the somber green
Of hemlocks turned to pitchy black
Against the whiteness at their back.
For such a world and such a night
Most fitting that unwarming light,
Which only seemed where'er it fell
To make the coldness visible.

John Greenleaf Whittier, 1807-1892

Bear Creek in Winter

Thank you for having cable so we can watch Beavis and Butthead cause we don't have cable at home.

- guest journal

Peanut Butter & Birdseeded Pine Cones

We all love the simplicity of feeding and decorating for our fine feathered friends, and it is so much fun for children - and for the child in all of us.

Pick the prettiest pine cones.
At the pointed end of the pine cone, tie a piece of raffia, leaving the ends about 6 inches long to hang from the tree. With a knife, spread peanut butter around the majority of the pine cone. Spread birdseed on a paper plate. Roll the peanut buttered pine cone in the birdseed.
(This is a child-friendly, messy project.)
Using a big square of cellophane, clear or colored, wrap the pine cone and tie it at the top with a raffia loop or bow.
Receivers of this delightful gift can just untie the cellophane and hang the cone on a favorite outdoor spot.
Don't be surprised if you are feeding the squirrels too!

Snow Day

"It snowed last night!"

No better words could fill the quiet air of morning.
"It snowed last night!" and nothing is the same.
Outside the window, rounded creamy shapes hide reality
And soft swirls around the lamp post
Speak of gusty wind.
Too tempting, snow draws children out like magic,
Their cries shredding the silence,
Their boot prints and snow angels many, and deliberate,
Their snowman co-ops presenting giants
Among the snowmen of the world.

Cedar trees are buried under wide
And drifted mountains,
And offer the best of all games:
Sliding without sleds, upside down,
To roll tumbling to a stop in mounded white drifts.
Bright, warm coats and hats and mittens
Show with sunny brilliance the woolen colors of winter.
Even so – even so, the cold creeps in
And suddenly the noses feel stiffened,
The fingers in the mittens are nipped blue with frost,
The toes are feeling numb and uncommonly large.
But little matter: Euphoric with freedom
From school's routine,
The running, playing, giggling, climbing,
Tunneling, tumbling children of winter play on,
Lost in the magic of four words, long wished-for:

"It snowed last night!"

Bette Milleson James

At the Inn we make sure we have every shape, color and size of marshmallows for the kiddos.

And I give them plenty!

Aaaah... Minty Cocoa

A Snow Bear will melt your *winter* heart and this delicious minty cocoa will warm your frosty fingers and toes!

These ingredients will serve four chilly bear-builders.

- ½ cup sugar
- ½ cup cocoa
- 1 teaspoon vanilla extract
- ⅓ cup hot water
- 6 miniature peppermint patties
- 4 cups milk
- 4 large marshmallows (and lots of little ones)

Stir together sugar, cocoa, vanilla and hot water in medium saucepan until blended.

Break peppermint patties into little pieces and drop into liquid.

Bring mixture to boil over low heat, stirring constantly.

Stir in milk and heat through. Pour into mugs, top with marshmallows, *and enjoy!*

Eliza's Homemade Graham Crackers

- ½ cup shortening
- ½ cup dark brown sugar
- ½ cup granulated sugar
- ½ cup honey
- ½ teaspoon vanilla
- 1 cup flour
- 2¼ cups whole wheat flour
- ¼ teaspoon salt
- ½ teaspoon baking soda
- 1 teaspoon baking powder
- ½ cup whole milk

In a large bowl, cream shortening and sugar until fluffy. Add honey and vanilla and stir well. In a separate bowl, sift the flour with the salt, soda, and baking powder. Add ⅓ of the flour mixture and ⅓ of the milk to the shortening mixture and mix thoroughly. Repeat 2 more times. Chill the dough for several hours or overnight.

Preheat the oven to 350°. Roll the dough on a floured board as thin as possible. Using a sharp knife, cut into squares. Arrange on a greased baking sheet and prick each cracker in several places with a fork. Bake for 10 to 15 minutes, or until golden brown. Makes about 4 dozen crackers.

Variation: For cinnamon graham crackers, sprinkle a mixture of sugar and cinnamon over the top of the crackers before baking.

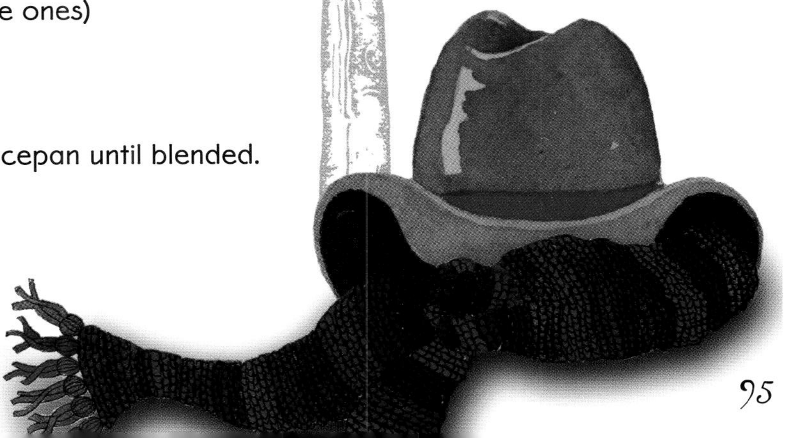

The grate had been removed from the wide
overwhelming fireplace,
to make way for a fire of wood,
in the midst of which was an enormous log,
glowing and blazing, and sending forth
a vast volume of light and heat;
this I understood was the yule log,
which the Squire was particular in having brought in and
illumined on a Christmas Eve,
according to ancient custom.

Washington Irving, 1783-1859

Hearthside

- Yule Log Tradition
- Yule Log Blessing
- Hearthside Basket
- Crunchy Apple Cranberry Crisp
- Holiday Dipped Candy Canes

Yule Log

Today's Yule Log, with its symbolic message of friendship

The warmth and light of ceremonial fire have met mankind's most fundamental needs from time immemorial, and the Yule Log has been part of those ceremonies throughout recorded history. The tradition took on new meaning when those who practiced it became Christian in their belief, and the Yule Log's ritual fire became a significant part of Christmas.

The burning of the log was not a simple matter in days gone by. First, it was unlucky to buy the log, but necessary to obtain it from one's own land or to receive one as a gift from a friend or neighbor. Second, it must be brought in on Christmas Eve, often decorated with ribbons and evergreens. The master of the house sprinkled the wood with oil, salt, and mulled wine, saying suitable prayers.

The log was lit with clean hands as a mark of respect, often by a young girl of the house. It was kindled with the cinders of the previous year's log, carefully preserved for this purpose.

If the log did not ignite immediately, misfortune would follow the family for the new year, so great care was taken to ensure an instant flame. Often, dry holly was placed under the log as fine kindling, along with the old cinders. At the first sign of flame, guests would toss small pieces of holly onto the fire to burn the troubles of the past year and to keep the flame burning until the log itself was well ignited.

Once burning brightly, the log had to be kept aflame for twelve hours without tending. Of course, ultimately, the log was intended to burn through all the twelve days of Christmas.

I love creative presentation so
I buy (from craft or hobby store) gold or clear cellophane by the roll.
Cut extra large for Yule Log and bundle with red or natural raffia at the top.
Attach your blessing.

Supplies:

Short full round logs
Approximately one foot in length, bark on and watch for logs that have a flat bottom so they won't roll while you are working on them. (You can notch bottom with saw, too.)

Scented wax or candle to drip on log
Orange and cinnamon spice are my favorites. I save old candles for these.

Sprigs of greenery-many varieties, *the more the better!*
I use a mixture of many trees at the Inn; blue spruce, fir, pines.

Cinnamon sticks, pine cones, twigs, berries, dried flowers
Everything must be flammable.

Sparkling sticks or pine cones
I buy these at a craft or hardware store.

Raffia and brown paper bags
Yule Log Blessing - copy our blessing, or write your own, onto brown grocery bag paper. Tear rather than cut, for a vintage look. Roll, tie, and attach.

Glue gun and several glue sticks

Directions:

1. Brush any excess dirt from your log.
2. With scented candle, drip wax so it runs down the sides of your log. It will show on each side and will smell wonderful.
3. Start with your longest pieces of twigs, attaching firmly with glue gun. Glue from center of log working out in both directions.
4. Layer your greenery, making log top full.
5. Glue and hold while setting. (Careful on fingers with hot glue!)
6. Add your remaining ingredients, tucking pinecones, cinnamon sticks and flowers into greenery.
7. Add more twigs if you like, with the center highlighted.

Yule Log Blessing

With this Yule Log,
we offer you
all these traditions:
warmth and light,
story and song,
food and fellowship,
and from our hearts,
the great gift and blessing
of friendship.
May your hearth be warm,
your feast be hearty,
your days be joyous,
and your hearts be at peace.

Feel free to copy our blessing to attach to your Yule Log gift.

Hearthside Basket

These are so very attractive sitting by your fire, whether it is gas or wood burning. We use them at all our fireplaces all year and we keep adding and embellishing. Use all or any portion of the following. Most can be collected by a walk in the woods, made or purchased from your local craft store.

Change the contents of your basket with the seasons...

Kindling or sticks of varying lengths

Greenery from spruce, fir or evergreens

Pinecones

Long matches (or fireplace lighter)

Newspaper folded in thirds (if you plan to start a fire)

Longer twigs, berries, leaves, holly

Fire starters

A winter quote (like the one below)

Light your fire and never fear
Life is made for love and cheer!

Old Arts and Crafts quote

Snow is back! Slept in this morning and nothing is better than waking up to the softness of a beautiful woman and the sound of the mountain creek outside. Life is good, very good.

- guest journal

It is important to make your basket look "overflowing." Add a potpourri you enjoy that could go into the fire or one that just makes the rooms smell good!

Crunchy Apple Cranberry Crisp

Filling:

4-5 large apples
  tart firm apples such as Jonathan or Granny Smith
⅔ cup flour
½ cup sugar
2 teaspoons cinnamon
1 cup cranberries

Topping:

1 cup oats
½ cup brown sugar
2 teaspoons cinnamon
½ cup granola
¾ cup chopped walnuts
3 teaspoons butter

Core and chop apples into chunky bite-sized pieces.

In a large bowl combine apples, flour, sugar and cinnamon until well mixed. Mix in cranberries.

Pour into deep 8-inch, well-oiled pan. Should be rounded and full.

In medium bowl combine oats, brown sugar, cinnamon, granola and walnuts. Cut in butter with pastry blender until mixture becomes mealy.

Spread topping over apple mixture evenly.

Bake at 350° for 35-40 minutes.

I have probably made hundreds of these for our guests; I make them at home while I watch TV and can almost do it with my eyes closed. There is a therapy to cutting apples, and the smell of this dish baking is heavenly. At the Inn we often place a small pitcher of milk alongside.

Holiday Dipped Candy Canes

20 small candy canes
8 ounces semi-sweet chocolate
8 ounces white chocolate

Line a baking sheet with waxed or parchment paper. Melt each chocolate separately in double boiler or microwave. Stir each often and be sure not to overcook.

Dip each candy cane in semi-sweet chocolate ⅔ of the way up the longest part of the cane.

Place on prepared cookie sheet to set (at least 10 min).

Once first dipping has set, dip each cane again, in white chocolate, covering ⅓ of the semi-sweet chocolate. Place on prepared cookie sheet to set.

This hideaway is breathtaking in winter! Now I know what peace is. Thank you so much.
- guest journal

Ancient pagan societies gave eggs as gifts in the springtime
as symbols of the natural cycle of death and rebirth.
Just as a chick hatches from its egg,
so does the earth as it emerges from the dead of winter.
The growth of spring starts the annual cycle anew.

While the Easter Bunny did not become
a popular custom until the late 1500s,
the practice of decorating eggs was firmly established
by the Middle Ages.
English records show that King Edward I bought 450 eggs
to be gold-leafed and gifted for Easter in 1290.

Gail's dad, Bob, and Aunt Mary Louise

The Chicken or the Egg?

Chickens, Chickens, Chickens

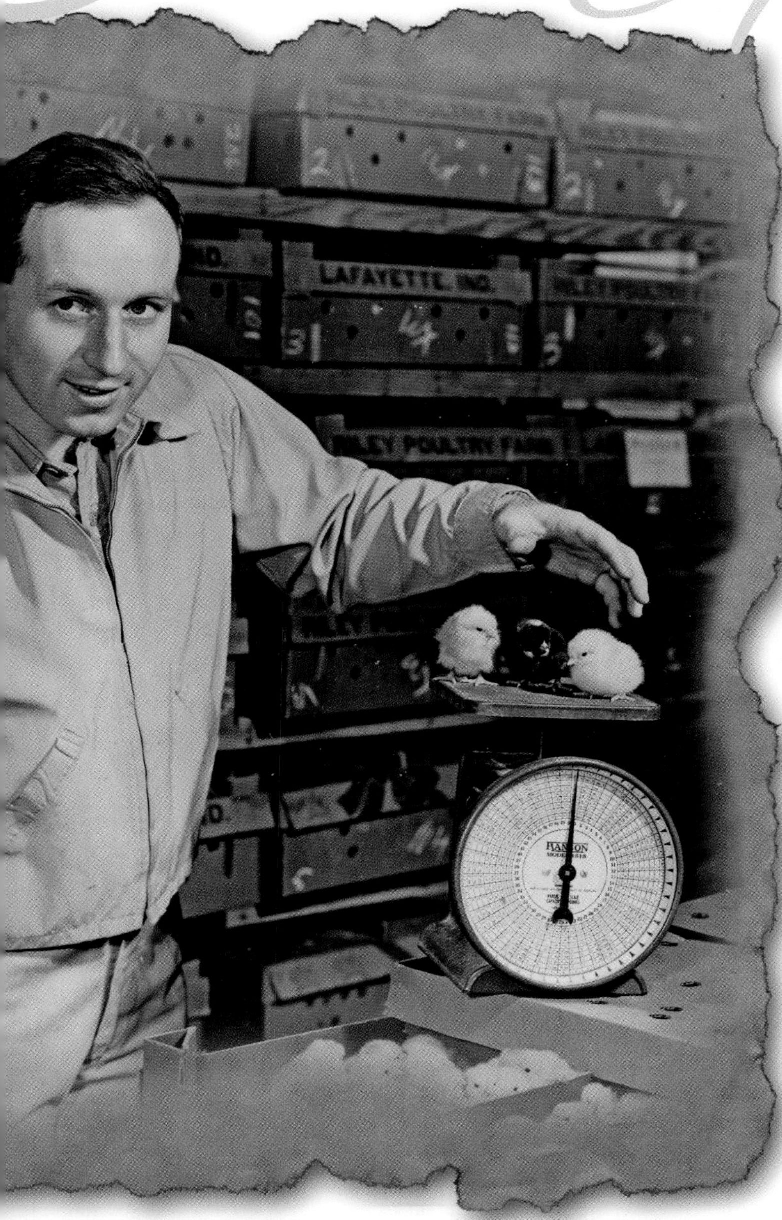

Gail's Dad, Bob Riley, largest turkey farmer in Indiana.

Which came first? To get an egg, you need a chicken, but to get a chicken, you need an egg! We had to start somewhere, so to get our eggs we ordered chicks from the Murray McMurray Hatchery catalog. What fun that was! The 24 little chicks arrived at the post office, and they were the sweetest little things! Delicate and tiny, they still had to be kept warm, carefully fed, and tended to. The odyssey was just beginning. My husband, Statz, built our chicken coop, I painted it with nursery rhyme motif, and each chicken has her own nesting area. He still says that each egg is worth about five bucks, after building the coop, feeding the brood, and laboring daily. It is Statz who is the wonderful "farmer"!

Although I had a bit of poultry in my blood, the basics escaped me, as I have learned they do most people. The hands-down biggest misconception is that the eggs can become chicks. Not true. The "facts of life" remain the same for chickens – an egg has to be fertilized by a male, called a rooster, to produce a chick. Sperm from the male fertilizes the eggs inside the hen. This must happen before a chick can start to develop inside an egg.

Female chickens, called hens, start laying eggs when they are about a year old. Before the hen starts to lay her eggs, she makes a scrape in the ground with her beak and feet. She pulls twigs, feathers, hay, and leaves around her. If one of the eggs rolls away, she pulls it back under her with her beak. The hen lays from seven to fifteen eggs in a clutch. She lays one egg a day. She does not start to incubate them (by sitting on them) until the last egg of the clutch is laid. Because of this, all the eggs start to develop and hatch at the same time.

The biggest delight has been with kids — collecting an egg, touching a chicken or feeding the chicks through the chicken-wire fence. Fun!

Eggs, Eggs, Eggs...$, $, $

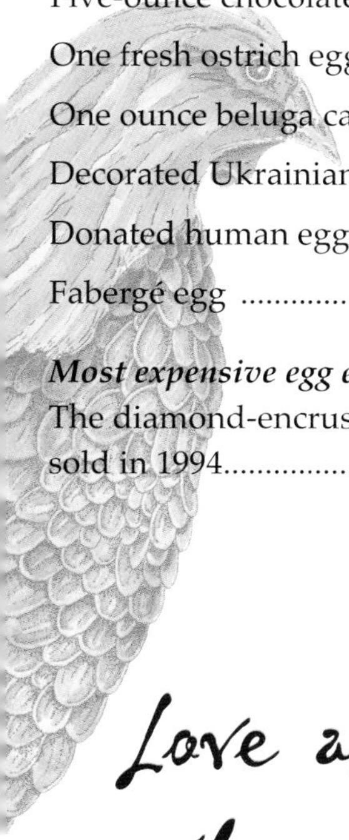

One dozen fresh jumbo chicken eggs	$1.22
One dozen fresh duck eggs	$4.00
One average-size blown goose egg	$1.50
One average-size blown ostrich egg	$9.00
Five-ounce chocolate egg	$7.50
One fresh ostrich egg	$10.00
One ounce beluga caviar	$95.00
Decorated Ukrainian egg	$195.00
Donated human egg	$12,000.00
Fabergé egg	$3,500-150,000.00

Most expensive egg ever sold:
The diamond-encrusted Fabergé "Winter Egg" sold in 1994 .... $5,600,000.00

Love and eggs are best when they are fresh.

Russian Proverb

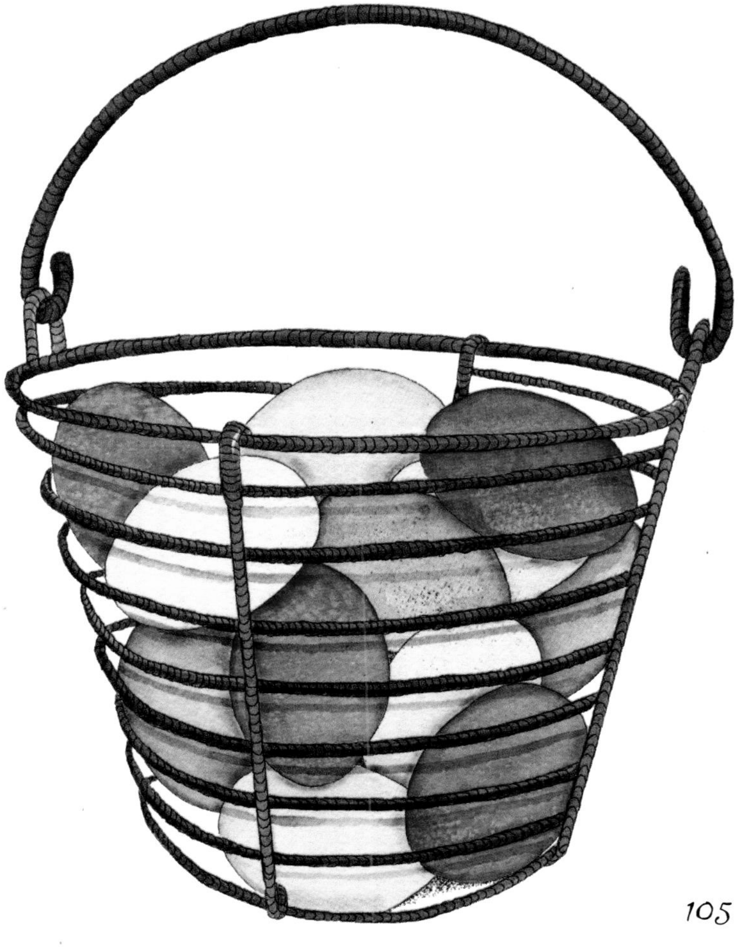

Breakfast Egg Strata

Basic Filling

3-4 cups day-old bread
6 eggs
2 cups milk
½ cup shredded cheese
1 teaspoon dried mustard
salt and pepper to taste

Preheat oven to 375°.

Grease a 9x13-inch baking dish and line with the torn, chunky bread.

Top with a variation of your choice.

Beat eggs with milk, dried mustard, salt and pepper. Pour over filling, sprinkle evenly with shredded cheese.

Bake for 50-60 minutes or until egg mixture is cooked through.

Choose one of the variations:

Cheesy Garden Vegetable

1 tomato, chopped or sliced
4-5 mushrooms sliced
½ cup fresh baby spinach leaves
3-4 asparagus spears cut into thirds
cheddar cheese

Benedict

½ cup Canadian bacon, chopped
3-4 asparagus spears cut into thirds
Monterey Jack cheese
Serve with hollandaise sauce

Southwest

1 small can chopped green chilies
1 tomato, chopped
1 tablespoon fresh cilantro
Combination of Cheddar and Jack cheeses

Note: You may prepare and refrigerate overnight before baking if you like. This method frees you up in the morning.

Our Egg Stratas ...

are and always have been the breakfast dish our guests love the most and "crave" when they are away. One of the beauties of this dish, especially for us, is that it's so very versatile and we can prepare it the night before, freeing us in the morning for all the additional preparations we must do to offer our memorable breakfasts.

The Strata is as good as the bread it begins with, so start with a wonderful bread – then add any of the endless array of ingredients to 'build' your Strata. Nothing smells as good as a strata baking, full of simmering fresh vegetables, meats and cheeses.

Each of our staff puts her own creative "mark" on her strata. A particular joy of mine is that this dish is often the very first that our younger staff members learn to make. The pride of serving their creations to our guests, and then most often to their families at home, just tickles them – and me.

Don't hold yourself back here. The Strata is similar to a good vegetable soup – it can be as specific as our recipes or you can add a bounty of your favorite ingredients or whatever you have on hand!

Remember, you make this the night before you wish to serve, so all the flavors seep into the bread. And you can relax and visit as your creativity bakes in the morning. A puffy hot strata is sure to satisfy your most discriminating family members and guests.

The Moms, Gail and Amy, with their chicks

At 20 and just home from a trip to Barcelona with his dad, Jaxon asked for his favorite dinner. Ham and eggs with white sauce is a simple and tasty dish. Just add veggies and cup of fruit for a well-rounded meal.

Jaxon's Blue Plate Special

4 hard-boiled eggs cut into large pieces

1 1/2 cup cubed ham (I buy one ham steak.)

White Sauce

2 tablespoons butter
2 tablespoons flour
Salt, pepper to taste
1 1/2 cup milk
1 tablespoon chicken bouillon

Heat butter in saucepan over low heat until melted. Blend in flour, salt and pepper. (I use a whisk to mix.)

Stir in milk and heat to boiling, stirring constantly. Boil one minute, add bouillon, ham and eggs.

Serve over split biscuits or toast points.

Serves 4.

Statz is the coop builder and the closest thing to a farmer here - the chickens owe him a debt of gratitude for the daily food, water and custom made "digs."

Our lusty rooster,
The Donald, didn't last long.
His six o'clock a.m. welcome didn't work
well for our road-weary guests.

Another 'Grate' Egg Idea

With your additional hard-boiled eggs from Easter (or any time) consider these:

Grate eggs into spinach salad with bacon.

Grate over our "Albino Gazpacho." *(page 56)*

Add to a potato salad.

Toss into an omelet for texture.

Keep whole eggs handy for teens on the go or for adults to enjoy with a Bloody Mary at brunch.

The Highland Haven Creekside Inn

of Evergreen, Colorado
proudly offers our
"home grown" **EGGS!**

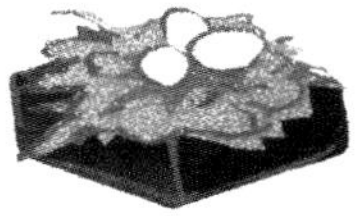

FRESH EGGS BROUGHT TO YOU DAILY BY:
The Girls!
Silver Laced Wyandottes, White Rocks, Rhode Island Reds, Buff Orpingtons and the Black Cochin.

Herbed Deviled Eggs

12 organic (cage free please!) large eggs

1 cup sour cream

2 tablespoons chopped chives *(Chives grow early and easily in your garden. We have a bed just outside our kitchen door for an easy grab.)*

2 tablespoons chopped parsley *(same growing suggestion)*

2 tablespoons your favorite mustard

1 tablespoon lemon juice

salt and pepper to taste

paprika to garnish

In a medium saucepan, cover eggs with cold water and bring to a boil on high.

Remove from heat and let stand for 15 minutes. Drain the hot water and run icy cold water over the eggs. Let them sit for 10 more minutes.

Peel eggs (good luck!) and cut in half lengthwise. Remove yolks to small bowl and add sour cream and remaining ingredients.

Mash and stir with a fork until smooth.

Fill egg whites with yolk mixture, garnish lightly with paprika and chill.

Irresistible, as well as a great source of protein!

Eggs and cheese are such good partners! You will see how many ways we put them together. Both are sources of complete animal protein and are great substitutes for meat. We had a family tradition in our home as I was growing up to have a "breakfast-like" dinner with eggs on Sunday nights - relaxed and easy for the cook and a nice break from the norm.

No traffic,
no sirens in the night.
No noisy streets.
No pollution.
No crime.
No stress.
Boy – do we miss
New York!
- guest journal

More Winter Recipes

We have a wonderful new breakfast menu of heart-warming comfort food for each season. For winter we love to serve our baked oatmeal with fresh berries, trifle with carrot cake, whipped cream, raisins, fruit, and nuts. And always I make our ever-popular winter bread puddings, as well as tarts and crisps loaded with cranberries and nuts.

Holiday Crunch Granola

3 cups regular rolled oats
½ cup whole almonds
½ cup pecan halves
½ teaspoon ground cinnamon
¼ teaspoon nutmeg
½ cup brown sugar
½ cup honey
½ cup water
⅓ cup oil
2 teaspoons vanilla
⅓ cup dried apricots
⅓ cup golden raisins
⅓ cup currants

Combine oats, almonds, pecans, cinnamon, and nutmeg in large bowl. Mix well.

In another bowl combine brown sugar, honey, water, oil and vanilla. Add to oat mixture, stirring to coat well.

Spread in baking pan.

Bake at 300° for 1 hour, stirring every 15 minutes.

Cool completely and then stir in dried fruit.

Store in airtight container.

Aunt Ruth's Hummel Futter

2 eggs beaten
2 tablespoons sugar
1 tablespoon flour
1 teaspoon baking powder
½ pound chopped dates
½ pound chopped nuts
2 oranges
2 bananas
Red cherries and whipped cream

Mix eggs, sugar, flour, baking powder, dates and nuts.

Bake at 375° for 30 minutes.

About one hour before serving, break the cake into bite-sized pieces in serving dish.

Top with sliced oranges and bananas, then with whipped cream and cherries on top.

Aunt Ruth discovered this recipe at a Hummel family reunion.

Pear-Cranberry Crisp

Streusel Topping

1 cup flour
1 cup brown sugar
1 cup quick cooking oats
½ cup chopped pecans
3 teaspoons cinnamon
2 sticks unsalted butter cut into chunks

Filling

12 ounces fresh cranberries
¼ cup sugar
¼ cup orange juice
5 Bartlett or Anjou pears, skins on, cored, 1″ chunks
2 tablespoons flour
1½ teaspoons ginger
1 teaspoon nutmeg

Heat oven to 350°.

Combine flour, brown sugar, oats, pecans, 1½ teaspoons cinnamon and butter in large bowl. Use pastry blender to cut in butter until mixture is crumbly. Set aside.

Cook cranberries, sugar and orange juice in saucepan until cranberries pop, about 5 minutes.

Place pears in large mixing bowl. Place 2 tablespoons flour, ginger, remaining cinnamon and nutmeg in sifter; sift over pears. Toss.

Stir in cranberries. Pour into buttered 9x13-inch baking dish. Cover with streusel topping.

Bake until fruit is soft and topping is golden, about 45 minutes.

Pear and Raisin Cobbler with Cheddar Topping

Filling

6 large Bartlett pears, peeled, cored and sliced
½ cup raisins
½ cup sugar
1 tablespoon water
1 tablespoon plus 1 teaspoon cornstarch
1 tablespoon lemon juice
½ teaspoon cinnamon

Topping

1½ cups flour
½ cup sugar
2 teaspoons baking powder
2½ tablespoons butter, softened
⅔ cup finely shredded sharp cheddar cheese
3-4 tablespoons milk
1 egg

Heat oven to 400°.

Butter a 2-quart shallow baking dish and set aside.

Combine all filling ingredients in a medium saucepan. Cook over medium heat until pears are hot and mixture is slightly thick, about 5 minutes; pour into prepared baking dish.

Stir together flour, sugar and baking powder in a small bowl. Cut in the butter with pastry blender until crumbly.

Stir in cheese, milk, and egg. Drop by spoonfuls over pear filling.

Bake for 25-30 minutes or until topping is set.

Best served warm.

Classic Tea Cookies

1 cup butter, softened
1 cup sugar
1 cup powdered sugar
2 eggs, beaten
1 teaspoon salt
1 cup vegetable oil
2 teaspoons vanilla
4½ cups flour
1 teaspoon baking powder
1 teaspoon cream of tartar

Cream butter and sugars.

Add eggs and salt. Beat well.

Beat in oil and vanilla.

Sift dry ingredients together and mix in. Makes a very soft dough.

Drop by scant teaspoons onto ungreased cookie sheet. Oil bottom of glass and dip into a dish of sugar. Flatten cookies on pan. Dip in sugar before every cookie.

Store in an airtight container.

Festive Cranberry Tart

2 envelopes of unflavored gelatin
½ cup cold water
6 cups fresh cranberries
1⅓-2 cups sugar to taste
1 cup red currant jelly
2 tablespoons cognac
1 10-inch tart pan with pastry pre-baked and cooled

Soften the gelatin in the cold water.

Combine the cranberries, sugar, jelly and cognac in a saucepan and cook over low heat for 10 minutes. Do not overcook or the mixture will become too watery; the cranberries should be soft but not bursting.

Remove from the heat and let cool slightly.

Stir in the gelatin and let cool completely. Pour the cranberry filling into the tart shell and chill for at least 1 hour.

Poinsettia Champagne

To each glass of champagne add…

1 teaspoon cranberry juice
½ teaspoon triple sec

Float 2 cranberries in each glass.

Riley's Scones

3 cups sifted flour
2½ teaspoons baking powder
½ teaspoon baking soda
½ cup sugar
1 teaspoon salt
¾ cup butter
¾ cup currants
1 cup buttermilk

Combine flour, baking powder, baking soda, sugar and salt in a large bowl. Then cut in butter with pastry blender and add currants, gradually adding buttermilk until dough clings together.

Turn onto floured board and form a ball. Press down, forming a disk that is 1 inch thicker in the center than on the edges.

Cut with a serrated knife into pie wedges. Brush tops with buttermilk and bake in 400° oven for about 15 minutes. Lightly sugar the tops if you like.

These scones should not be browned.

Cranberry Clafouti

3 cups fresh cranberries
1½ cups cranberry juice or water
6 eggs
1 cup plus 2 tablespoons sugar
6 tablespoons flour
1 cup plus 1 tablespoon milk
¾ cup heavy cream
¾ teaspoon vanilla
pinch of cinnamon

Cook cranberries in juice or water over low heat for 5 minutes. Drain, reserving juice. Boil down juice until reduced to ¼ cup, about 7 minutes.

Combine the eggs, sugar, flour, milk, cream and vanilla in a blender and blend at high speed for 1 minute, scraping down sides once. Or beat with mixer until smooth. Stir in reduced juice.

Use cooking spray on a 9-inch baking dish or quiche pan. Spread the cranberries evenly over bottom. Pour batter evenly over berries. Sprinkle with cinnamon. Bake in 400° oven until puffed and golden, about 40-45 minutes. Serve warm. Serves 6.

Gift from a wandering artist, 1987

Anne's Apple Strudel

Dough

1 small egg
1 teaspoon salt
⅓ cup oil
⅔ cup very warm water
2½ cups sifted flour

Apple Mixture

2 sticks melted butter
¼ pound vanilla wafers, crushed
2 to 3 pounds thinly sliced apples
2 cups sugar
¼ teaspoon cinnamon

In a mixing bowl, beat well egg, salt, and oil. Add ⅔ cup very warm water and continue beating until frothy.

Gradually add flour, beating with mixer until little bubbles form.

Place on floured bread board and knead, adding more flour until dough is firm.

Place in large flat pan, cover with plastic wrap and set in warm place one hour.

Roll on floured cloth, then stretch until paper thin.

Brush dough with melted butter.

Sprinkle wafer crumbs.

Spread apples and sugar mixed with cinnamon.

Roll up as for jelly roll. Place in greased pan.

Bake in preheated 375° oven for an hour.

I travel extensively for my job.
It is such a pleasure to find a cozy spot
surrounded by nature.
- guest journal

Cinnamon Streusel Coffee Cake

¼ cup butter
¾ cup sugar
1 egg
1½ cups flour
2 teaspoons baking powder
½ teaspoon salt
1 cup milk
1 teaspoon vanilla

Topping

1 cup brown sugar
3 tablespoons flour
2 teaspoons cinnamon
4 tablespoons butter
½ cup walnuts or pecans, finely chopped

Preheat the oven to 350°.

Spray a 9x9-inch pan with non-stick cooking spray.

In a medium bowl, cream the butter and sugar; beat in the egg.

Sift together flour, baking powder, and salt in a separate bowl. Add to creamed mixture alternately with milk.

Stir in vanilla.

Pour blended mixture into prepared pan.

To make topping: in a small bowl, mix together sugar, flour and cinnamon. Cut in butter with pastry blender. Spoon half over batter and swirl.

Spoon remaining topping over batter and sprinkle with nuts.

Bake for 40 minutes until lightly browned and filling is set.

Come bring, with a
Noise my merrie,
Merrie boy
The Christmas log to
The firing
While my good dame,
She bids ye all
Be free,
And drinke to your
Heart's desiring.

With last yeere's Brand
Light the new Block,
And for good success
In this spending
On your psalteries play,
That sweet luck may
Come while the log
Is at ending.

Robert Herrick, 1591-1674
"Yule Log Song"

Caramel Dipped Chocolate Apples

1 dozen lady apples
1 16 ounces package of caramel candies
6 ounces semi-sweet chocolate pieces
6 ounces white chocolate
1 cup finely chopped walnuts
Cookie Sticks

Wash and completely dry lady apples. At the top of each apple, press the cookie sticks into each apple about two-thirds of the way in. Spray baking sheet with non-stick spray and set aside.

Prepare assembly line for dipping:

Melt caramels according to directions on packaging. Set pan for first station of line. Place chopped nuts in small bowl for second station.

Melt chocolates in double boiler (separately) or microwave. Be sure to stir each often during melting process and do not overcook. Spoon each chocolate into freezer bags and snip one bottom corner (leaving 1/16 of an inch hole for applying the chocolate). These will be for the third and fourth stations.

To prepare each apple:

Dip apple in caramel, roll in nuts, lace with semi-sweet chocolate then white chocolate and place on greased pan to set.

The Inn Through the Seasons

Everything in this room,
from the music and the chocolates
and the wonderful comfy bed,
to the rippling sound of
Bear Creek through the window,
is calling me to come back.
Thank you for this peace.

- guest journal

The Inn Through the Seasons

Tour of the Inn

- The Dailey Cabin
- Gardener's Cottage and Guest Rooms
- Hillside Cottages and Junior Suites
- Creekside Cottages and Evergreen Suite
- Blue Spruce Cottages and Fireside Loft

The mountains are calling,
and I must go.

John Muir, 1838-1914

The Dailey Cabin

A Little About the Cabin

Skirting the eastern edge of downtown Evergreen, at the crook of a sharp curve in Bear Creek across from Sheep Head's Rock, sits what old-timers say is the first cabin ever built in Bear Creek Canyon. The historic Dailey Cabin, which today anchors the Highland Haven Creekside Inn, was named for its original owner, John L. Dailey, Sr., a printer from Ohio who co-founded the Rocky Mountain News. According to two of his children, John Jr. and Grace, their father built the one-room, hand-hewn log cabin in 1884.

The Daileys owned the cabin for nearly 70 years, during which time many members of the extended family enjoyed the rustic cabin and its natural surroundings. One of John Sr.'s daughters, Anna Emily, discovered a rare spurless columbine flower near the cabin around 1890. The flower, a variation of the official Colorado state flower, was not seen again until the 1970s in nearby Indian Hills. Juanita Dailey, granddaughter of John Sr.'s brother William, was known to live in the cabin with her mother, Mabel, as late as 1954.

Other summer cabins were soon built near the Dailey Cabin, including one owned by E.B. Field, president of Mountain States Telephone and Telegraph Company. Around 1925, Field sold his cabin to the Beecher family, who enjoyed the retreat until it was sold in the early 1950s.

At some point during the 1950s, the Dailey and Beecher properties were combined, the cabins were expanded, and a no-frills summer-only motel called the Highland Haven was born. Over the next decade or so, the motel welcomed travelers during the summer months, and was used to house the area's teachers during the school year.

It remained a motel when current owners Gail Riley and Tom Statzell and their partners bought the property in 1979. When Riley and Statzell assumed sole ownership in 1987, they began to transform the motel into the luxurious, year-round bed and breakfast inn it is today.

In 1996, they began restoring the Dailey Cabin, recreating a 19th-century ambience with updated comforts. Statzell removed the low ceiling and the cheap paneling covering the walls, exposing 30-foot expanses of log. He built or restored all of the cabin's woodwork, including the beautiful hardwood furniture, while Riley decorated in the Mission and Arts & Crafts styles. Today the Dailey Cabin is the site of the inn's delicious breakfasts, a space where guests relax and read, and the ideal spot for business and social functions.

Throughout the years and the changes, one thing has remained consistent about this distinctive property among the tall pine trees along Bear Creek: It has always been a haven for resting, rejuvenating, and communing with nature.

A Little from Eliza

Back in 1884, John Dailey longed for a cozy cabin, a mountain retreat, where he could escape the pressures of the big city. He built his cabin in Evergreen, Colorado, of hand-hewn 30-foot logs. They were joined together with the square nails that were common at the time and with chinking that was mixed on the property with stream water. The cabin, which took 12 hours to reach from Denver, became an oasis for the busy man who co-founded the Rocky Mountain News.

The Dailey cabin is still standing today, and in good shape, thanks to Tom Statzell and his wife, Gail Riley, proprietors of the Highland Haven Creekside Inn. Tom is the designer, builder, and refurbisher of the property. He hand-peeled the log beams in the cabin with a drawknife. He built the stone walls that wind through the grounds. And he raised the roof and refurbished the Dailey Cabin. Now fully restored and furnished with original Stickley and Mission pieces, the exquisite log structure is used for conferences, fancy brunches and private parties. "The cabin speaks to a calmer time," says Gail.

And that is, perhaps, the essence of most of our cabin dreams. We invite you to dream of your own highland haven.

Eliza Cross, Publisher, *Log & Timber Style Magazine*

"It (the cabin) would have been something anyone could have had," says John Stinley, director of the Hiwan Homestead Museum. "There was a sawmill right on Bear Creek almost at the cabin's back door. The builder would have cut the logs, chained them together, attached them to a horse or oxen, and 'snaked 'em' to the site. With ten or a dozen people, he could have put the walls up in a day."

If walls could talk!
We found these cut-outs
behind the wall board when we
refurbished our "Champagne Room."
All are actors, actresses, and
opera singers,
according to our historical experts –
one is a Barrymore!

Climb the mountains and get their good tidings.
Nature's peace will flow into you as sunshine flows into trees.
The winds will blow their own freshness into you,
and the storms their energy, while cares will drop off like autumn leaves.

John Muir, 1838-1914

Springtime

Spring at 7000 feet in the Rocky Mountains means the birds (today I spotted the finches and nuthatches), the snow, the bulbs all co-mingle. One day we wear t-shirts and the next the snow gear is out again. But spring always shows promise... that soon I will tend to the dozen gardens that are still dormant and need much attention.

It is a short season for us; not until June will our mass of lilacs bloom, and then boom! It will be summer. We celebrate the awakening of Mother Nature. She will be hard on us with spring snowfalls, but they will offer us the healthy flow of our beautiful Bear Creek. Our sweet ducks, Herb and Lois, will return. Our dogs Lola and Rowley have already had fun romps with the elk in the creek. Evergreen will clean off the soil of the winter and will spruce up to welcome the endless days of bright sunshine and mountain-style fun.

Gardener's Cottage

Nothing is overlooked in this sumptuous setting: a decadent king canopy bed in front of a moss rock fireplace, a 46-inch TV, a steamy two-person Jacuzzi and use of our luxurious velour terry bathrobes. Your own handsome sitting room is filled with deep rich woods and a leather sofa and wet bar. Enjoy picture-postcard views from your private deck. Splurge here; it's worth it!

Let us be grateful to people who make us happy; they are the charming gardeners who make our souls blossom.

Marcel Proust, 1871-1922

Guest Rooms

Select a cozy room with one or two beds and a private entrance on the garden level of our beautiful main lodge. All our amenities are just for you in these comfy homes away from home. With private baths, our tastefully decorated hideaways are reasonably priced and conveniently located for easy access to a luscious breakfast at the lodge.

The pure glamour
of romance changes an ordinary day
into the stuff of dreams.

The wonders of
the Rocky Mountain High
have now been revealed to us
as we languish in
your magnificent abode and bed!

– guest journal

He wrote:
This place really does feel magical.
I love the stream being
right outside the cabin.
I loved it so much that it became
the inspiration to ask the woman
I love more than life to be my wife.
The chairs by the creek made
a perfect cuddling and preparing spot.
It was almost as beautiful and perfect
as my new fiancée.
Oh, and she said "yes"!

She wrote:
Last night the sweetest, kindest,
most loving man I have ever met
asked me to spend my life with him.
Although I would have said "yes"
no matter where he asked me,
this place made the perfect setting!

- guest journal

The sculpture Intimacy *by Denver artist Reno Carollo*
graces our creek front for lovers and all to admire.
Purchased through "Art for the Mountain Community,"
it was originally part of Evergreen's annual Sculpture Walk
and now is a permanent piece at the Highland Haven.

Summertime

The days are longer. The sun is higher in the sky and the snow has long left the banks of the creek that runs the length of the Inn. The summer season puts us in "high gear" with guests enthralled with Colorado and our Highland Haven. We have the rooms at their very best; fresh flowers grace their tables, herbs garnish our signature sumptuous breakfasts, and we are delighted to live each bountiful day in such a beautiful place. We are thankful and we pinch ourselves. This is a great life and we are ready to share it.

Hillside Cottages

Spacious and so very "Colorado Chic," these cottages are ideal for the celebrating couple or for the family. Ask for the cottage with the hot tub stepped down from the master bedroom – it's extravagantly comfortable and convenient! Hillside Cottages have two bedrooms and a wonderful main room featuring a fireplace and a wet bar. Our opulent, luxurious king and queen beds, velour bathrobes, and tub/shower bathrooms are all for your convenience and comfort. Warm, woodsy vaulted ceilings with log beams, hand-crafted elements throughout, and absolute privacy will make this your hillside home.

Junior Suites

Each lovely two-bedroom suite has a private bath with shower, a convenient wet bar, and a sitting room with French windows or a walk-out balcony to offer amazing mountain views that will calm your soul. The suites are tastefully furnished for your comfort and pleasure in our mountain hideaway.

Stars of the summer night!
Far in yon azure deeps
Hide, hide your golden light!
She sleeps! My lady sleeps!

Henry Wadsworth Longfellow, 1807-1882

Earth and sky, woods and fields,
lakes and rivers,
the mountain and the sea,
are excellent schoolmasters,
and teach some of us more than
we can ever learn from books.

John Lubbock, 1834-1913

Thank you to the Highland Haven
for making my life a bit easier
by doing the dishes, making the bed, cooking.
Our third year of marriage was spent apart -
husband in Iraq and I tending to 2 children,
full-time job and a house under renovation.
This has been a wonderful break.
Even though our time was short we do plan
on coming back for another romantic time.
Thank you for everything.

- guest journal

Thousands of tired, nerve-shaken,
over-civilized people
are beginning to find out that going
to the mountain is going home;
that wildness is necessity;
that mountain parks and reservations
are useful not only as fountains of
timber and irrigating rivers,
but as fountains of life.

John Muir, 1838-1914

The dog who licked my hand –
Was he just hungry, or
Did he just have good taste?

Our Little Lola

Autumn

As the cool weather approaches I rediscover the beauty of this season at the Inn. Crisp mornings, lower sun, aspens turning golden; and so many varieties of birds are back: evening grosbeaks, stunning woodpeckers, and chirpy little nuthatches of many colors. We return to a controlled (sometimes) calm after frantically fun summer activities. The welcomed new flavors of breakfast bring back our sweet-smelling baked oatmeal, homemade granolas and the "farmyard" pecan waffles that we prepare for the weekends. (You will love!) I will be making my personal favorite – a crisp with Colorado-grown apples and cranberries. It smells heavenly while baking and tastes even better.

Have a look at our "Wild West Dinner Party." Perhaps it will inspire you to plan a gathering on a chilly autumn evening.

Do check in, settle in and savor the splendor of this season at Highland Haven. We will all be here to welcome you –including our sweet canines, Rowley and Lola.

Creekside Cottages

Crafted in high style, each of these classic Colorado cottages offers intimate Ralph Lauren luxury in a four-poster honey pine queen bed, within a setting of warm wood tones, log beams, a convenient wet bar, and a lovely bath with shower. Bear Creek, just off the deck, will lull you out of the 21st-century and into times past as you luxuriate in front of a Vermont casting gas fireplace.

Evergreen Suite

This extremely spacious suite features a king master bedroom, another king in the second bedroom, and a private indoor hot tub with use of our cushy terry velour bathrobes. A massive wood-burning stone fireplace and full kitchen make this one truly a home away from home. The private deck, with spectacular views of Bear Creek and the rock outcropping, brings the Rockies to your very door. The lavish warmth of this special suite will make you want to stay forever.

It was thirteen years ago today
that I asked my wife
to marry me in this very room.
We are so glad to celebrate our
12th wedding anniversary
in the very same room.
Thanks so much for giving us
a romantic place
to reaffirm our vows of love!

- guest journal

A place of peace, calm and healing.
A pure joy in every sense.
A wonderful place to finish my book on Search & Rescue.

- guest journal

The air cools,
leaves change color,
and year after year we travel
from near and far
simply to see the spectacle.
Anyone who calls this
a land of cynics
has never watched us
watching the leaves.

This most evocative of seasons brings nature's invitations to brisk walks and simmering soups, to hot bread bowls and the slower cooking and slower moving life of seasonal change. While supper's in the oven, give yourself the gift of fall's fresh and bracing air with a walk through the dried beauties that surround you, and gather them in. Free for the taking are all the things you need to make beautiful flower boxes, yule logs, hearthside baskets, cornucopias, and other cold-weather dried delights. Wherever you live, there are leaves, small branches, intricate weeds, wildflowers, sometimes pine cones or honeylocust shells... all lovely, all versatile, all free.

Wintertime

Winter at the Inn brings a calm I welcome. The holiday décor, the winter menus, and nature's new visual delights are stimulating – yet every little thing is slower and wrapped in a cocoon only winter brings. My favorite times are those when I hike or hunt for nature's treasures in our woods by the inn. This week I pulled sapling firs and spruce only inches high, that are crowded out by larger trees, to transplant into our flower boxes. I gently peeled rich green moss from the banks of the woods to layer at the base of each little tree.

Blue Spruce Cottages

The Blue Spruce Cottages are our most celebrated accommodations for unforgettable romance or luxury business. Log beams offer ambience, and a moss rock gas fireplace spreads warmth at the foot of the most divine king bed. Amenities include a wet bar, a beautiful over-sized bath with jetted tub and use of our sumptuous velour bathrobes, and an LCD flat screen television. Each cottage has sublime décor and access to a courtyard for relaxing in the Colorado air. These lavish cottages are steeped in romance and ready to satisfy your Highland Haven cravings of all kinds.

It's snowing and cold
and peaceful.
What a beautiful place to
spend a night away from the
hustle and bustle of daily life.
We wish we'd known about
this place years ago!
We can't wait to come back.
Thanks for a wonderful stay!
- guest journal

Fireside Loft

Our loft accommodation is absolutely unique. Bold architecture with high ceilings, wood floors, and a grand living room featuring leather furniture, a personal bar, and a beautiful gas fireplace await the traveler. Massive windows frame beautiful views of Fern Gulch. The absolutely dreamy master bedroom offers a king sleigh bed and custom mosaic tile bathroom, with the warmth of our cozy velour bathrobes at hand. Fireside Loft is capped off with a private canopied outdoor hot tub – elk watching is excellent! This very special suite is extremely secluded, private, and personal.

One of the very best things about winter is the anticipation of spring and all it brings – new birds singing, our ducks returning to Bear Creek, bulbs and flowers popping up from the ground.

Snowfall

Snow plastered wet
Testing wiper thrusts
And blotting nighttime vision.

The narrow wooden bridge,
Smaller in the dark and blizzard,
Welcomes us at midnight.
Dim office lights
Affirm place:
The Highland Haven
Alerting late visitors,
Wanting to tuck in
Beneath the sheets and quilts.

Soft white flakes
Pillowed all 'til morning.
Lying over roofs and road,
Virgin it was at six
And photographed while lying deep.

Virgin cream lost soon
By gravelly shovel scoops and throws
From walk to wayside drift
Along the way
To our room and others,
Making the trudge to sumptuous brunch
Easy enough for us who stay.

Really from our window view
We need no camera to mentally imbed
The handsome bridge
Across the rock-strewn stream,
Each artifact capped in white
Yet room for rushes,
Brushes, eruptions, pools
And branches interrupting
Along the broken, headstrong run
To destinations below
The snow and happening gorge.

Paul Sheckler, a favorite guest of the inn, March, 2006

Keep close to nature's heart...
and break clear away, once in awhile,
and climb a mountain
or spend a week in the woods.
Wash your spirit clean.

John Muir, 1838-1914

May golden slumbers
kiss your eyes and
May calm await you
when you rise.

Pillow tag quote

Best Dressed Guest Room

- Just for Fun
- Add to the Comfort
- Suggestions for Perfection
- Bedside Welcome
- Kind Considerations
- Pillow Tag Quotes of Note

Guest Rooms

Nothing is so satisfying to an innkeeper as offering a beautiful, luxurious, inviting guest bedroom. We live to please our guests, and all our creativity pours into our efforts to do so. As important as a recipe in our kitchen at the inn, this little recipe for our Best Dressed Guest Room is easy to follow and filled with goodies. The best part is that, unlike a luscious cake or casserole, the room can be used again and again – you have only to replace the small amenities and clean till it sparkles.

Music is for the soul of mankind, so we play a CD of beautiful, soft music (or whatever you think your guests might like, if you know them). Set the player to 'repeat' so they walk in to calm, pretty music. Have a favorite assortment of tunes and a variety of musical styles available to them.

For a romantic touch, place a welcome "Pillow Tag" or a hand-written welcome note, either with candies on the pillow or on a side table — or offer fruit, a power bar, or cookies for the more practical-minded guest.

Be My Guest!

Recipe for your Best Dressed Guest Room

1 comfy bed
1 good chair
Great lighting
Sparkling, flattering mirrors, one full-length
1 closet or place for your guests' belongings and clothes
1 CD player

Arrange all with an eye to ambience and comfort. Then start thinking like an Innkeeper and spoil your guests, being sensitive to the extras, the creature comforts, the personal luxuries:

Lovely fresh flowers around the room and at bedside

Beautiful, luxurious bedding
(clean and simple cotton sheets to avoid sheet sensitivity)

Backup blankets in the closet, or folded at the foot of the bed

Perfect pillow choices (feather, foam or firm)

Several convenient toiletries (a little kit of minis)

Fresh-smelling candles, lightly scented and well contained

A soft, plush throw for those snugly daytime naps

Eye candy – family photos, delightful art, photos of you with your guest

And add your own favorite luxury

With all these in place, simply set the lights, start the music, light the candles, and create that home away from home we all adore.

Best Dressed Guest Room

Just for Fun

*be the concierge as well as the innkeeper.
A busy and independent guest is the best guest!
At our Inn, we have printed lists of our
"favorites" placed in the rooms – lists for
summer, for winter, for romance, for kids...
For example, our romance list includes
spa offerings, antiques shops to browse,
intimate restaurants, the best views to find,
winery or brewery offerings,
shopping fun, walks around Evergreen Lake,
and other romantic temptations.*

Add to the Comfort

***of your beautiful bedroom
with these variations on the recipe:***

A conveniently located TV and remote control

A good fan to use as a noise buffer
and for air circulation

A telephone to assist your guests who may face
cell phone connection challenges

Robes and slippers –
generic size; you can't cover them all.

A "Do not disturb" sign for the doorknob, a nice
reminder for kids or for time-zone sleep deprivation

A well-lighted makeup area
(a solution for the busy bathroom)

Suggestions for Perfection

Splurge on a dozen quality hangers and hang them in the front end of the closet, with plenty of space for hanging your guests' clothes. If space is cramped, give what space you can and offer a foldable luggage rack; just leave it in the closet until you put it out for their arrival. Leave empty a couple of top dresser drawers, smelling sweet and clean.

Ahead of time send your guests an email with a link to the local chamber of commerce web site so they can look into all sorts of activities your town offers: museums, art shows, cultural events, fairs, films, shopping, wineries, outdoor activities, and specialties only your region can offer.

Place a few brochures about local wonders near the comfy chair, if a tourist is what your guests want to be. Local transportation schedules will help if you have guests in your home, and you aren't on vacation while they are!

Bedside Welcome

Good bedside alarm clock

Good reading lamp, 100 watt bulbs

Juicy bedtime reading – trashy or classy magazines

Nice tissue box

Comfort films - DVDs of feel-good movies if a player is available in the room

Kind Considerations

Consider the possibility of guests' allergies – if you have pets in your home, have your guest room especially clean, and air it out for a dander-free space. At the Highland Haven, clean, fresh pet-free and smoke-free rooms are a priority.

In Colorado's extra dry climate, we provide humidifiers for those who need them. Space heaters in winter will take the chill of our mountain air from your highland hideaway.

Always appropriate is a supply of bottled water – room temperature is fine, or put bottles on ice in a pretty bowl for your guests' arrival. (Water is especially important in Colorado for sea-level guests with high-altitude physical challenges.) In a basket, tray or drawer, provide these thoughtful relief amenities for minor discomforts:

Lip balm
Aspirin for travel headaches
Hand lotion (a must in Colorado and other dry parts of our country)
Benadryl for allergies

If your guests happen to include Mom and Dad or Gramma, consider their personal needs and comfort, remembering that quiet and privacy may be high on their lists!

Menu

It was so much
like home,
I made my own bed.

- guest journal

Pillow tag quotes of note:

"May your night be filled with the simple pleasures of a starry night, crisp mountain air and the sounds of Bear Creek to lull you to sleep."

Or make a simple tag wishing "Sweet Dreams"

Full many a glorious morning
have I seen
Flatter the mountain-tops
with sovereign eye,
Kissing with golden face
the meadows green,
Gilding pale streams
with heavenly alchemy.

William Shakespeare, 1564-1616

Sweet Dreams from the Highland Haven

Listing of Recipes

Springtime

Summertime